Bead One, Pray Too

Bead One, Pray Too

A Guide to Making and Using Prayer Beads

Kimberly Winston

MOREHOUSE PUBLISHING
An imprint of Church Publishing Incorporated
HARRISBURG—NEW YORK

Morehouse Publishing, 4775 Linglestown Road, Harrisburg, PA 17105

Morehouse Publishing, 445 Fifth Avenue, New York, NY 10016

Morehouse Publishing is an imprint of Church Publishing Incorporated.

Interior and cover photography: Andy Lyons
Stylist: Sue Banker
Cover design: Brenda Klinger
Interior design: Beth Oberholtzer

Library of Congress Cataloging-in-Publication Data

Winston, Kimberly, 1964–
      Bead one, pray, too : a guide to making and using prayer beads / Kimberly Winston.
         p.   cm.
      Includes bibliographical references.
      ISBN 978-0-8192-2276-3 (casebound)
      1. Beads—Religious aspects.   2. Prayer.   3. Rosary.   I. Title.
BL619.B43W56   2008
203'.7—dc22

2007038258

Printed in Malaysia
08 09 10 11 12 13   10 9 8 7 6 5 4 3 2 1

For my friend Sandy Olson,
whose life was an inspiration because of her great faith
and the way she put it into practice.
I miss you.

CONTENTS

ACKNOWLEDGMENTS

I am more grateful to the following people than I can ever hope to tell them in words, written or spoken. Without any one of these people, this book might not have come to be: Nancy Fitzgerald, my wonderful editor at Morehouse, who guided me with strength and purpose. Diane Connolly, David Gibson, and Ari Goldman, colleagues who read chapters and offered both their vast experience and gentle feedback. Phyllis Tickle, who made me believe I can do anything. Sue Banker and Andy Lyon, who captured the beauty of the beads in photographs. Dorothy Perez, who drew the illustrations, and Steve Riley, the best publicist going. And my husband, Terry, who makes the very act of writing possible.

INTRODUCTION

When holy and devout religious men
Are at their beads, 'tis much to draw them thence,
So sweet is zealous contemplation.

—WILLIAM SHAKESPEARE, *RICHARD III*

When I was a little girl, sometimes after school I used to cross the street from our apartment building and sneak into the cool, dark sanctuary of Blessed Sacrament Catholic Church. I use the word "sneak" because I had the mistaken idea that I shouldn't go into a church that wasn't Protestant, as I was. But I loved Blessed Sacrament, with its statues of serenely gazing saints, its many Marys in blue robes holding chubby babies, the rows upon rows of flickering flames in red glass holders, and the golden glow of the altar candlesticks. There was a great hush about the place that was a welcome respite from the New York City streets outside. But more than anything, I loved the rosaries I saw clasped in the hands of the old Polish and Irish ladies scattered through the pews. In the dim light from the stained glass windows, their small beads winked and twinkled as they clicked through the women's knobby old fingers. The women seemed to whisper to their beads—I couldn't hear what they said—and kissed them quickly, almost furtively, before slipping them back into their pockets. I didn't know what those beads were or how they were used, but I knew I wanted some. They were pretty and sparkly and there was mystery attached to them, something I knew had to do with the big crucifix at the front of the church. But I wasn't sure what it was and I was too scared to ask a priest and I never thought to ask my own pastor.

I was a Methodist and we didn't have rosaries. We had confirmation Bibles and that was about it. As I grew up and learned more about other religions, I discovered how the Catholic rosary was used and why. I admired those who had the dedication and faith to pray with it daily. But somehow I didn't feel I could take up the tradition of counted prayer. It just didn't seem to *belong* to me.

Then, about two years ago, I wrote a feature story about a growing number of people combining various hobbies with their faith—sewing prayer quilts, knitting prayer shawls, painting icons, stitching skull caps. More than one of the groups I came across in the reporting made something they variously called an Anglican, Episcopal, or Protestant rosary. What, I wanted to know, could that be? Didn't only Catholics have rosaries? A quick search on the Internet showed me I was wrong. There was information about this new rosary on the websites of Episcopal, Methodist, Lutheran, and Presbyterian churches. Most people who use this new rosary credit its creation to an American Episcopal priest who taught others how to use this ancient form of contemplative prayer. Many have formed groups that make rosaries and give them away, while others make them and explore their use in personal and group prayer.

The Anglican or Protestant rosary, these websites say, is a simple thing—thirty-three beads and a cross. Its great beauty lies not in the attractiveness of its beads, but in that *there is no right or wrong way to use it*. Instead of one officially sanctioned set of prayers, like the Catholic rosary, or a couple of traditional ways of praying with it, like the Hindu mala, this form of rosary can be used to pray *any* prayers you are drawn to—from the prayers of the liturgies and Daily Offices of the church to personal poems of self-expression. You can pray one word on each bead, like a mantra—perhaps the name of God or the word "peace"—or you can recite more complicated expressions of faith from the Scriptures or other literary sources. You can memorize the prayers or read them. You can say them aloud or in your heart. You can pray with your eyes opened or closed. You can pray on your knees or at your job. You can do anything with it.

That is not to say that there are no guidelines for using the Anglican or Protestant rosary. But it is so accommodating to our needs, our goals, our own individual spiritual quests that the many possibilities need some rounding up and explaining.

The same day I learned about this new rosary, I made a quick one. I threaded a needle, strung some beads I had left over from another project in the order I saw described on the websites, tied a knot, and settled down on my bed, my dog at my feet. Unsure about this very un-Protestant–seeming thing, I selected very simple prayers—the Jesus Prayer ("Lord, Jesus Christ, have mercy on me") and the prayer of Julian of Norwich ("All shall be well and all shall be well and all manner of thing shall be well"). Then I just started to pray, slipping the hard, round beads through my fingers one at a time, one for each repetition of the prayers.

I did not expect that this handful of beads would set me on a path of prayer that would change the way I think about God and my relationship to him. But it did. After a week or so of praying with the beads every day, I began to feel my mind click off in the middle of the recitation. The almost constant chatter that runs through my head—my perennially long list of chores and tasks and worries—began to recede. In its place came a stillness, a place where there is only me, my beads, and my longing for God. When I end my session with the beads, I come away feeling more serene within the landscape of my life. I don't sweat the small stuff as much as I used to. I don't feel alone, but as if I had just spent time with a good friend, one I will see again the next day when I take up the beads again.

All of this took practice and patience. It didn't miraculously happen in a single session. But it happened, and I never expected it to. Now I have that rosary I longed for as a child. In fact, I have made more rosaries than I can count, keeping many and giving others away. I use them every day, taking them with me everywhere I go, a set for every purse and vehicle I own. I have learned many prayers by heart and have written other, more complicated ones in a journal I keep with my rosary. I yearn for the time each day I will spend with my beads—often on one of my walks or just before bed. They carry me beyond myself and my troubles and preoccupations to a quiet place where I can just sit and *be*. I hope this book will help others see how they, too, can make this spiritual practice their own.

Some Terminology

Christian prayer beads, the main subject of this book, have many names: the Catholic rosary is also called the Marian or Dominican rosary, and the Anglican rosary is also known as the Episcopal or Protestant rosary. In this book, I will use the term "prayer beads" to refer to the general category of strung beads used to count prayer, and the word "rosary" to refer to strung beads used to count Christian prayer. If I need to distinguish between the different kinds of rosaries, I will add the adjectives "Anglican," "Lutheran," "Protestant," "Orthodox," or "Catholic."

How to Use This Book

In this book, we'll take a three-part journey. In the first part, I'll introduce the prayer beads of the world's religious traditions and describe what they are made from and how they are used. Then we'll take a closer look at the Catholic rosary and the Anglican or Protestant rosary it gave birth to. We'll delve into the history of these and other forms of Christian prayer beads to place them within the context of the world's religious traditions. We'll look at how these Christian rosaries are used and how they can enrich our individual spiritual practices by drawing us closer to God through counted prayer. In the second part, we will look at the many prayers that can be said on the rosary, taking the words of Jesus, Mary, and other saints and putting them at our fingertips and in our mouths. Lastly, we will learn how to make different prayer beads through simple bead stringing techniques, and we'll explore the symbolism we can give them through the materials we choose. I hope that you will come to fall in love with this great prayer tool as I have.

After reading the first section, you may want to jump to the third section and make your own rosary so you can try the prayers gathered in the second section. Or, you may want to skip making a rosary altogether and jump to chapter eleven and buy one from one of the resources listed there. Catholic rosaries can be found in most religious bookstores and many Episcopal churches and cathedrals with stores have Anglican rosaries available for sale.

And a caution—the purpose of this book is not to encourage anyone to pray the way I do. Your prayer life is your business, not mine. Rather, it is to share this simple prayer tool and the doors to contemplation it can open. My hope is that others will find it as rewarding as I have.

PART ONE

BEADS OF FAITH

Islamic subhahs and a Hindu mala.

CHAPTER ONE

A HISTORY OF BEADS AND PRAYER BEADS

Just as there is one thread
And on it are woven breadthwise and lengthwise
Hundreds of thousands of beads
So is everything woven unto the Lord

—GRANTHA SAHIB 2352, NAM DEV, INDIAN POET,
THIRTEENTH-FOURTEENTH CENTURY CE

There is something about human beings and a craving for adornment. We have an innate longing for the attention and status beads and jewelry bestow. The oldest known beads, made of teeth and shell, were found in a French cave and date back thirty-eight thousand years to the Neanderthals. But because most early beads were made of organic materials—wood, seeds, clay, and the like—finds like these are rare. Today, beads are made to last— most are mass-produced in factories in Japan and the Czech Republic. But there are still many individual artisans crafting fine handmade beads in glass, clay, ceramic, silver, and other metals.

Our instinct for decoration is matched by our instinct for religion. Every culture, no matter how modest or great, no matter how ancient or recent, has some set of religious beliefs. Perhaps it is only natural, then, that beads and religion should have such a long association. Many scholars write that the majority of beads made by our ancestors served some sort of spiritual purpose. Some were worn as a sign of station or class, often signifying the role of priest or shaman, while others served as talismans, protection against the uncertainties and dangers of life. In the Far East, ancient Tibetans made etched *dZi* beads of agate, giving them the patterns and symbols of the Bo religion, an early precursor to Buddhism. These are now known as "Buddha's eyes" and are supposed to have mystical powers to bring good fortune. Another such surviving bead is the "eye bead," a blue and white bead that resembles a staring blue eye believed to protect against evil. Today, it is not uncommon in Turkey and its surrounding countries to find both Muslims and Christians who carry these along with their Islamic prayer beads and Catholic rosaries or Orthodox prayer ropes.

No one is certain when people began counting prayers on beads. Many scholars believe the Hindus of ancient India were the first to engage in the widespread use of prayer beads. The first known use of prayer beads dates to a third-century BCE statue of a Hindu holy man draped with beads hung by devotees. Buddhism, another product of ancient India, probably borrowed prayer beads from Hinduism. As traders and travelers came through the Indian subcontinent, and as Indians ventured beyond their own borders, the practice of counting prayers on strings of beads spread to other parts of the world and soon, to other faiths. Today, counting prayers on beads is one of the most common spiritual practices, performed in places as different and distant as India and Indiana and by people of faiths as varied as Buddhism and Wicca. It is a practice that links the world's believers in diverse faiths, joining them in a shared longing for the divine, just as the beads themselves are bound together by a single thread or cord.

Prayer Beads in World Religions

Hinduism

Hinduism is the oldest of the world's religions, taking gradual shape from various local traditions scattered throughout India. In Hinduism, Brahma is the creator of all and has many aspects, including Shiva, the destroyer, and Vishnu, the preserver. Hindu prayer beads, called a *mala*, or "rose" in Sanskrit, have 108 beads, usually made from seeds and worn around the neck. Devotees of Shiva favor malas made from *rudraksha* seeds—Sanskrit for "Shiva's eyes"—while the followers of Vishnu make theirs from the *tulsi* plant, a kind of basil. The number 108 is sacred to Hindus, as it corresponds to the number of Brahma's names. The recitation of these names, called *namajapa*, is a sacred practice. Three other Indian-born religions—Buddhism, Jainism, and Sikhism—feature the use of 108-beaded malas, evidence of the sharing and blending of religious traditions and the common desire of the devout to count prayers on beads.

Buddhism

Buddhism arose in India about 500 BCE. Like the Hindus, the Buddhists call their prayer beads a *mala*, and it, too, consists of 108 beads. In Buddhism, the number 108 represents the number of sins people can commit and the number of virtues they can aspire to. Many Buddhist temples have 108 steps which the faithful climb to worship. In Zen Buddhism—the Japanese form of the

He who has learned to pray has learned the greatest secret of a holy and a happy life.

WILLIAM LAW

faith—108 bells are rung at the new year, marking the number of temptations humans must overcome to achieve nirvana, the ultimate goal of Buddhism.

The Buddhist mala is often made from the wood of the bodhi tree, the type of tree the Buddha was reclining beneath when he achieved enlightenment, an ideal state of total detachment and peace. As the faith spread across Asia, the mala was crafted from other materials, including bone, amber, and semi-precious stones. A Buddhist mala has beads in three sizes. The bulk of the beads—105 of them—are the same size, with one larger bead and two smaller ones at the end. These beads signify the "three jewels" of Buddhism: the Buddha himself, his teachings (*dharma*), and the monastic way founded by the Buddha (*sangha*). A Buddhist uses a mala to count repetitions of the mantra "Om mani padme hum," considered the "true words" of the Buddha and which roughly translate to "The jewel of the heart of the lotus." The person reciting grasps a bead between the thumb and second finger, which represent the body and the spirit. Buddhists believe the repetition of this mantra puts one on the path to enlightenment.

Judaism

Judaism is the only world religion that does not have a tradition of prayer beads. Some scholars say they are forbidden by Jewish law as a pagan practice. But Jews do have a form of counted prayer in the *tallit*, the four-cornered prayer shawl worn by men (and some women, in the more liberal forms of Judaism) for morning prayers, *Shabbat*, or Sabbath, services, and the High Holy Days of Rosh Hashanah and Yom Kippur. The tallit have a border with knotted fringe, known as *tzitzit*. The purpose of the tallit is to hold the tzitzit, which God, in the Torah, instructs the Jewish people to wear so that they might not forget the commandments:

God wills that men should pray everywhere, but the place of His glory is in the solitudes, where He hides us in the cleft of the rock, and talks with man face to face as a man talks with his friend.

SAMUEL CHADWICK

Speak to the Israelites, and instruct them to make for themselves fringes on the corners of their garments throughout the ages; let them attach a cord of blue to the fringe at each corner. That shall be your fringe; look at it and recall all the commandments of the Lord and observe them, so that you do not follow your heart and eyes in your lustful urge. Thus you shall be reminded to observe all My commandments and to be holy to your God. (Num 15:38–40, Hebrew-English Bible[1])

Today, there are centuries-old techniques and rules for the tying of the tzitzit. Each tzitzit consists of eight strands of thread. The tallit maker wraps one strand around the others seven, eight, eleven, and thirteen times, with a knot in between each grouping of wraps. These numbers are rich in religious significance. Some say assigning these numbers to their corresponding letters in the Jewish alphabet spells the name of God. Others say adding and multiplying them in a certain way equals the number 613, the number of laws in the Torah. Whatever their meaning, they are an integral part of Jewish spiritual life, as many Jews touch the tzitzit and their knots at designated portions of their prayers.

Christianity

The very word "bead" comes from the Anglo-Saxon word *bede*, which means "prayer." The first mention of Christians and counted prayer is found in the third-century writings of the Desert Fathers and Mothers, who carried pebbles in their pockets and dropped them, one by one, as they said their prayers. Eventually, these pebbles were strung on a cord and carried. A Belgian museum claims to have a string of prayer beads that belonged to Saint Gertrude of Nivelles, a seventh-century abbess. In the eleventh century, Lady Godiva of Coventry—she of the legendary naked horseback ride—left a string of prayer beads in her will to a monastery she and her husband founded.

---

1. New York: Jewish Publication Society, 1917.

Today, the most commonly used form of Christian prayer beads is the Catholic rosary, which we'll look at in detail in chapter two.

In Eastern Orthodox Christianity, the devout use a prayer rope called a *komboskini* in Greek, and a *tchotki* in Russian. Instead of beads, these often have knots, usually thirty-three, fifty, or one hundred, and are made of wool, to represent the flock of Jesus. Eastern Orthodox prayer ropes are usually black, a symbol of one's sins, and instead of a crucifix, they usually have a knotted cross. The Orthodox most frequently recite the Prayer of the Heart, also called the Jesus Prayer, on their prayer ropes: "Lord, Jesus Christ, have mercy on me, a sinner." The supplicant holds the prayer rope in the left hand, freeing the right to make the sign of the cross. The prayer rope is never worn—that would be a sign of ostentation—and is always carried. No one is certain how the prayer rope developed, though it most likely evolved from the Desert Fathers' and Mothers' pebbles. Legend attributes its creation to Saint Anthony, the father of Orthodox monasticism. It is said that Anthony tied a leather rope with a knot every time he prayed in Latin *Kyrie Eleison* ("Lord have mercy"), but that Satan would come and untie the knots. Anthony then devised a way to tie the knots with seven wraps and crossings of the rope, so that each knot held within it the sign of the cross. The devil, it was said, was unable to bear the sign of the cross and was held at bay. Today, Orthodox prayer ropes are still tied in this intricate fashion.

Islam

Muslims believe the Prophet Muhammad, the founder of their faith, once said, "Verily, there are ninety-nine names of God, one hundred minus one. He who enumerates them would get into Paradise." In the pages of the Qur'an, the holy book Muslims believe was revealed to Muhammad in the seventh century, these names cover virtually every characteristic of God, or Allah, from "Most

Every great movement of God can be traced to a kneeling figure.

Dwight L. Moody

Merciful" to "The Avenger," and from "The Giver of Life" to "The Bringer of Death." Muslims believe that to recite these names is to invite Allah's blessings. "O God," Muhammad is believed to have said, "I invoke You with all of Your beautiful names." Many Muslims count all these names on sets of prayer beads called *subhah*, an Arabic word which means "to exalt." Subhahs come in strands of thirty-three, sixty-six, or ninety-nine beads, numbers that make it easy to keep track of the names.

Traditional Islamic prayer beads are round and are bound together with a larger, tubular lead bead and a tassel. Sometimes the tassel has two beads dangling from it as well. They can be made from wood, olive seeds, plastic, ivory, or clay. The tassel is called the *shahed*, or witness.

Muslims use the subhah after each day's five set prayer times, but are also free to use them whenever they want. And there is some flexibility in their prayers. Some Muslims recite *subhan'Allah* ("glory be to God") thirty-three times, *alhamdou'LillAh* ("praise God") thirty-three times and *Allahu Akbar* ("God is the greatest") thirty-three or thirty-four times, the last time upon the tubular bead. Some Muslims might repeat the Islamic call to prayer, which sounds from the world's mosques five times a day, calling the faithful to turn toward Mecca, the Muslim holy city:

> *Allahu akbar*
> God is great
> *La Ilaha ila Allah wa Mohamadun rasul Allah.*
> There is only one God and Mohammad is his prophet.

Muslims also use the subhah during the *hajj*, the pilgrimage to the holy city of Mecca all faithful, able-bodied Muslims must make at least once, using it to recite the names of God as they circle the Ka'ba, the large black sacred cube Muslims believe is the center of the universe.

Prayer the church's banquet, angel's age,

God's breath in man returning to his birth.

GEORGE HERBERT

Not all Muslims use the subhah. Followers of the Wahhabi school of Islam shun them in the belief that the Prophet Mohammad never used them, but counted his prayers with his fingers or with date seeds.

Baha'i

The Baha'i faith was founded in the mid-1800s in present-day Iran by a Persian holy man known as Bahá'u'lláh. Bahá'ís recite *Alláh-u-Abhá*, a form of God's name, ninety-five times a day. Baha'i prayer beads consist of some factor of ninety-five, usually nineteen of the same kind of bead with an additional five different beads hanging from the circle. They are usually made from wood, stone, or pearls. Some have a tassel and a nine-pointed star, the emblem of the Baha'i faith.

Neo-Paganism, Earth-Based and Goddess-Based Religions

No one can say for sure where the practice began, but today many Wiccans, Asatruar (believers in the ancient Norse religion), Druids, and followers of other earth-based and goddess-oriented faiths are making and using prayer beads for their individual and corporate practice. Some scholars of contemporary religions think that some Neo-Pagans (a blanket term for those who follow the many contemporary forms of ancient, pre-Christian faiths) are borrowing Catholic practices many may have been raised with before becoming Neo-Pagans. Other scholars say the fact that Neo-Pagans are codifying and counting prayer is a sign that these new religious movements are maturing. Whatever the reason, anecdotal evidence shows that more Neo-Pagans are using prayer beads, as the number of websites and new books dedicated to pagan prayer beads is on the rise. Some Neo-Pagans adapt a traditional Catholic rosary, removing the cross and replacing it with a more earth-

---

Our whole being must be in our praying; like John Knox, we must say and feel, "Give me Scotland or I die."

E. M. BOUNDS

oriented emblem, such as a fertility goddess, a tree, or a five-pointed star. Some also borrow traditional Catholic rosary prayers, but rewrite them with a focus on the goddess. Tirgereh is a Seattle-based Wiccan I met when I was writing a newspaper story about Neo-Pagans and prayer beads. She has made the Catholic rosary part of her practice since she was a college senior and now writes and shares her own prayers for it with others. One of them, which she calls "The Daily Elemental Rosary Prayer," begins like this:

> The day has begun, the time of resting at end
> as I gather and prepare to go forth
> I take this time to pray and remember:
> it is not alone do I wander
> it is not alone do I search
> it is not alone do I explore
> it is not alone do I live
> For I am surrounded with the love of the Mother
> And I am blessed with the bounty of the Father.

There are almost as many forms of prayer beads as there are religions. How can they help build a richer, fuller prayer life for those who feel called—as I did as a little girl—to learn about and use them? To discover this, we must first look more closely at the Catholic rosary, the main form of Christian prayer beads used today.

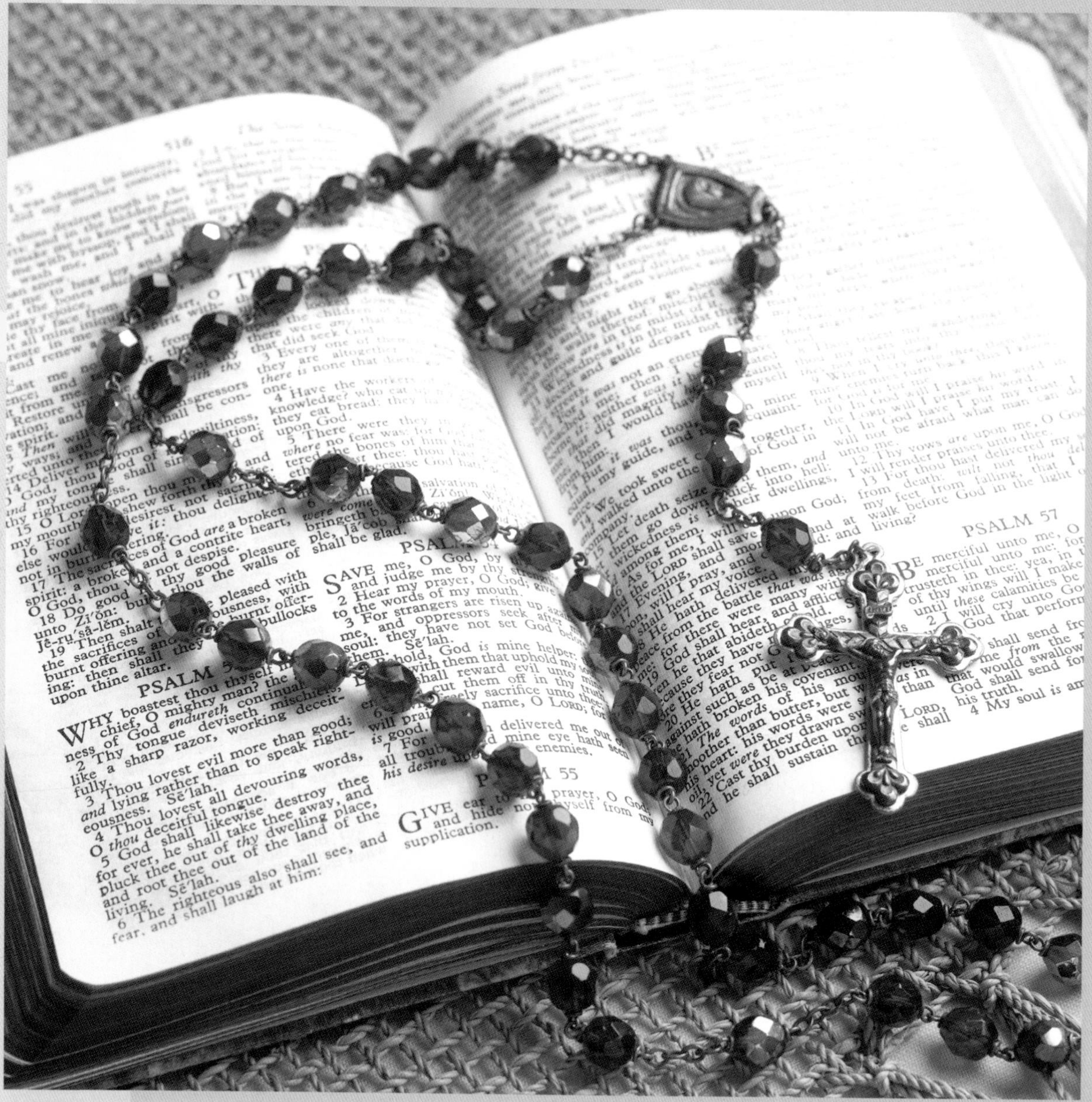

The Catholic Rosary.

CHAPTER TWO

THE CATHOLIC ROSARY

The Rosary has accompanied me in moments of joy and in moments of difficulty. To it I have entrusted any number of concerns; in it I have always found comfort.

—POPE JOHN PAUL II, *THE ROSARY OF THE VIRGIN MARY*

If I ask you to think of a rosary, you are most likely to conjure up an image of the dozens of beads connected with little links of chain and leading to a crucifix used by Catholics. You may even know that "Hail Mary, full of grace, the Lord is with thee" begins one of the main prayers of this rosary, recited by millions of Catholics worldwide every day.

Protestants may be uncomfortable using the Catholic rosary. For many, their faith tradition does not include praying to the Virgin Mary or to the saints and they may prefer to directly address Jesus and God. But to fully plumb the depths of the Anglican rosary and other Christian prayer bead practices, we must first understand the Catholic rosary. For one thing, the newer Christian rosaries are largely based on the Catholic rosary, both in form and function. There is also a long and rich tradition of prayer and contemplation associated with the Catholic rosary that other Christian rosaries, because they are new, have not had time to accrue. Protestants can learn much from Catholics when it comes to praying on beads.

The History of the Catholic Rosary

There is a beautiful story surrounding the origin of the Catholic rosary. In the thirteenth century, a thirty-three-year-old priest named Dominic was working to win converts in the heart of southern France. Alas, he was having little success. One day, he was complaining of this to the Virgin Mary in a prayer. Suddenly, the Virgin appeared before him. "Wonder not that you have obtained so little fruit by your labors," she told the startled future saint. "You have spent them on barren soil, not yet watered with the dew of divine grace. When God willed to renew the face of the earth, He began by sending down on it the fertilizing rain of the Angelic Salutation. Therefore, preach my Psalter composed of one hundred and fifty Angelic Salutations and fifteen Our Fathers, and you will obtain an abundant harvest." And she handed the astonished Dominic a rosary.

It's a lovely tale, and one that has been approved by thirteen Catholic popes despite the fact that there is no documentation from that time linking Dominic, founder of the Order of Preachers, or the Dominicans, to the rosary. And as we have already seen, people were using stones and seeds to count their prayers for many years before Dominic. A more likely explanation is just as captivating. Scholars believe the Catholic rosary was developed during the Middle Ages as a way for laypeople to engage in extended prayer. At the time, priests, nuns, and monks performed the Divine, or Daily, Office, which are set

Mary places in our hands a weapon for peace: the rosary. It is a weapon that every man, woman and child can take up.

M. Basil Pennington

prayers, based on the Psalms, sung at certain times of the day and night. Traveling orders—monks and holy men who worked outside the walls of a monastery—followed the breviary, a more truncated form of these prayers. For the common people—who were almost all illiterate—something simpler was required.

The first solution was to have the faithful recite all 150 Psalms in a single sitting. But that was too much for the average layperson to remember, so the Psalms were divided into three parts, allowing the devout to recite only fifty psalms in one session.

But even this was not simple enough. How many of us today could remember fifty psalms? So it became the practice to say the "Our Father"—the Lord's Prayer—150 times. If time or circumstances made it necessary, this could be reduced to one hundred or fifty Our Fathers. Keeping track of how many psalms or other prayers were said required a counting device, so a set of beads—with fifty, one hundred, or 150 beads—was settled on, and the beads became known as *Pater Nosters*, Latin for "Our Fathers." In London, an entire street of artisans crafted these beads on what came to be known as Pater Noster Row and the rosary became known as "the poor man's psalter."

The "Hail Mary" prayer assigned to most of the beads on the Catholic rosary in use today appeared in the fifteenth century. Again, for reasons that are not entirely clear—perhaps because it was shorter, perhaps because its plea is simple and direct—it became very popular and replaced the Our Fathers on most of the beads.

Also by the fifteenth century, the practice of praying the rosary while meditating on events in Christ's life became a common and codified practice. It was developed by Dominic of Prussia, a Carthusian monk, who highlighted fifty events in Christ's life for contemplation during the recitation of the rosary.

Dominic said the idea came to him in a vision in which he saw a tree with fifty leaves, each one representing a different episode in the gospel. Dominic's innovation was to assign each Hail Mary prayer and bead its own episode, such as Christ's birth, Christ's baptism, and Christ's death. But remembering fifty of these, too, proved too difficult for laypeople, and by the sixteenth century, the number of episodes was shortened to fifteen. This five-hundred-year-old practice of contemplating these mysteries while praying the Catholic rosary survives to this day.

The Mysteries of the Rosary

At the heart of the Catholic rosary lie the "mysteries," small kernels of wonder that form the foundation of the Christian story. The mysteries are drawn from the New Testament, mostly from the Gospels. There are fifteen mysteries divided into three groups of five each, and those who pray the Catholic rosary focus on one group of five at each rosary session—one for each decade, or set of ten beads, on the main circlet of the rosary. The groupings celebrate different periods of Christ's life. The first, called the Joyous Mysteries, come from the Gospel of Luke, and focus on Christ's birth and early life:

- the Annunciation (Luke 1:26–38)
- the Visitation (Luke 1:39–45)
- the Nativity (Luke 2:6–20)
- the Presentation in the Temple (Luke 2:22–39)
- the Finding in the Temple (Luke 2:41–52).

The next group, the Sorrowful Mysteries, come from Jesus' last days on earth:

- the Agony in the Garden (Mark 14:32–42)

- the Scourging (Mark 15:15)

- the Crowning with Thorns (Mark 15:16–20)

- the Carrying of the Cross (Luke 23:26–32)

- the Crucifixion (found in all four books of the Gospels).

Finally, the Glorious Mysteries surround the days just after Jesus's death and include stories of his mother's death not found in the Bible:

- the Resurrection (Luke 23:56–24: 12)

- the Ascension (Acts 1:6–11)

- the Pentecost (Acts 2:1–17)

- the Assumption of Mary

- the Coronation of Mary.

In the last century, Pope John Paul II, for whom the rosary held a special meaning, added five Luminous Mysteries, also known as the Mysteries of Light. These are all drawn from the public ministry of Jesus—something the first three sets of mysteries neglect. John Paul II called these the Mysteries of Light because they show Jesus as the light of the world through his teaching, his words, and his example. The Luminous Mysteries are:

- the Baptism of Jesus (Matt 3:13–17)

- the Marriage at Cana (John 2:1–11)

- the Sermon on the Mount (Matt 5:1–10)

- the Transfiguration (Luke 9:28–36)

- the Last Supper (Mark 14:22–25).

Give time to the rosary.

REPORTEDLY SAID BY AN APPARITION OF THE VIRGIN MARY AT MEDJUGORIE

John Paul II added another innovation by suggesting that the person praying speak aloud the name of each mystery before beginning each Our Father prayer, thereby announcing the mystery to be contemplated on the next set of decade beads. He also recommended a short silence after the announcement, and before the Hail Marys, to allow the full image and impact of the mystery to seep into the believer. Doing this, he promised, will prompt "the mind to be lifted up toward the Father," the ultimate goal of the rosary prayer.

John Paul II had still one more update for the rosary. For centuries, it was a Catholic custom to meditate on the different sets of mysteries at times corresponding to the seasons of the church. The Joyous Mysteries were contemplated from Advent to the start of Lent, the Sorrowful Mysteries during the forty days of the Lenten season, and the Glorious Mysteries were said during the rest of the year. Another tradition was to divide the mysteries up among the days of the week, with Mondays and Thursdays dedicated to The Joyful Mysteries, Tuesday and Friday to the Sorrowful Mysteries, and Wednesdays, Saturdays, and Sundays to the Glorious Mysteries. When the Luminous Mysteries were put into practice, the Joyful Mysteries were moved to Mondays and Saturdays, leaving Thursdays for the new mysteries. The mysteries and their corresponding days now look like this:

- Sunday—Glorious Mysteries
- Monday—Joyful Mysteries
- Tuesday—Sorrowful Mysteries
- Wednesday—Glorious Mysteries
- Thursday—Luminous Mysteries
- Friday—Sorrowful Mysteries
- Saturday—Joyful Mysteries

The rosary is an excellent prayer, but the faithful should feel serenely free in its regard. They should be drawn to its calm recitation by its intrinsic appeal.

POPE PAUL VI,
"MARIALIS CULTUS"

How are Catholics—or anyone else—to meditate on a scene from Jesus' life while remembering the prayers and counting them at the same time? Pope John Paul II suggested the use of icons, or other pictures and representations of these scenes. In his inspiring book *The Rosary*, Garry Wills, a Pulitzer Prize–winning historian and lifelong Catholic, takes John Paul II's words to heart and examines all the mysteries through the art of Tintoretto, the sixteenth-century Italian painter who depicted many scenes from the gospel. The result is an eye-opening lesson in how to pray with a simple set of prayers and a string of beads while contemplating some of the greatest wonders of the faith. Scores of artists, both the famous and the unsung, have been inspired by the events in the mysteries, and gazing upon them can spark a deep meditation. You can find many fine examples on postcards, prayer cards, or small plaques at Catholic and other religious bookstores.

The Catholic Rosary and the Anglican Rosary

Think of the Catholic rosary as the Anglican or Protestant rosary's older sibling. For one thing, there is a family resemblance. Both consist of a circle of beads with a short line of beads extending from the bottom. Both end with a cross. But while the Anglican rosary consists of thirty-three beads, the Catholic rosary has fifty-nine. The Anglican rosary has four "weeks" of seven beads each, while the Catholic rosary has five "decades" of ten beads each. Both have beads separating these groups from each other. The Catholic rosary almost always has a crucifix—a cross bearing the image of the crucified Christ—while the Anglican rosary usually has a bare cross. There is also usually a small medal of the Virgin Mary or Jesus on the Catholic rosary, linking the circle of the decades to the short string of beads.

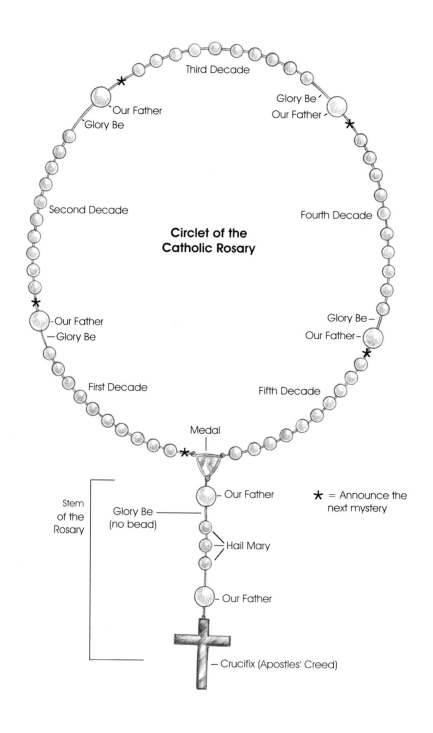

Third Decade

Glory Be
Our Father

★ Our Father
Glory Be

Second Decade

Circlet of the
Catholic Rosary

Fourth Decade

★ Our Father
Glory Be

Glory Be
Our Father ★

First Decade

Fifth Decade

Glory Be
(no bead)

Medal

★ Our Father

Stem
of the
Rosary

Hail Mary

★ = Announce the
next mystery

Our Father

Crucifix (Apostles' Creed)

*You give but little
when you give of your
possessions. It is when
you give of yourself
that you truly give.*

KAHLIL GIBRAN

Praying the Catholic Rosary

Praying the Catholic rosary is like embarking on a long, circuitous trip, both through the prayers and in contemplation of the mysteries, through the New Testament. Some of the prayers, such as the Apostles' Creed and the Lord's Prayer, will be familiar to most Christians, and they're included here with the wordings used by the Catholic Church.

The Creed

To begin the rosary, make the sign of the cross, using your right hand to touch your forehead, chest, left, and right shoulders. Then grasp the crucifix and recite the Apostles' Creed:

> I believe in God, the Father almighty, creator of heaven and earth.
>
> And in Jesus Christ, his only Son, our Lord, who was conceived by the Holy Spirit, born of the Virgin Mary, suffered under Pontius Pilate, was crucified, died, and was buried. He descended into hell; the third day he rose again from the dead; he ascended into heaven, sits at the right hand of God, the Father almighty; from thence he shall come to judge the living and the dead.
>
> I believe in the Holy Spirit, the holy Catholic Church, the communion of saints, the forgiveness of sins, the resurrection of the body, and life everlasting. Amen.

The Our Father

Move to the first bead above the crucifix and recite the "Our Father," also known as the Lord's Prayer. Catholics do not recite the last line most Protestants say, "For thine is the kingdom, and the power, and the glory for ever and ever. Amen."

In the simple prayer of the rosary beats the rhythm of human life.

JOHN PAUL II

Our Father, who art in heaven,
Hallowed be thy name
Thy kingdom come
Thy will be done
On earth as it is in heaven.
Give us this day
Our daily bread,
And forgive us our debts,
As we forgive our debtors,
And lead us not into temptation,
But deliver us from evil.

The Hail Mary

Next come a set of three beads. On each of these, recite a "Hail Mary" prayer. Tradition holds that this set of three prayers represents the three theological virtues of faith, hope, and love that Paul speaks of in First Corinthians. They can also represent the Trinity: the Father, Son, and Holy Spirit.

> Hail Mary, full of grace, the Lord is with thee. Blessed art thou among women and blessed is the fruit of thy womb, Jesus. Holy Mary, Mother of God, pray for us sinners, now and at the hour of our death.

The Glory Be (The Doxology)

There are no beads dedicated to the Glory Be prayer. Instead it is said in the small spaces after the three Hail Mary beads on the stem and between the last bead of each decade and the next Our Father bead. The prayer is based on Jesus' words in Matthew 28:19: "Baptize them in the name of the Father and the Son and the Holy Spirit."

To recite the Rosary is nothing other than to contemplate with Mary the face of Christ.

JOHN PAUL II,
"THE ROSARY OF
THE VIRGIN MARY."

Glory be to the Father, and to the Son, and to the Holy Spirit, as it was in the beginning, is now, and ever shall be.

Praying the Decades

This is the center of the Catholic rosary, its main path. It is the place where, through a repetition of simple prayers and a focus on the life and deeds of Jesus we can enter into a deeply prayerful and contemplative state.

On the last bead before the medal, recite another Our Father. This prayer goes with the first set of decades. Skip over the medal for now, and grasp the space between it and the first decade. Before you begin praying the decade, announce the first of the five mysteries assigned to this day's recitation. Pause a moment, as John Paul II suggests, to meditate on its meaning, and then begin the decade's Hail Mary prayers, saying one on each of the next ten beads. At the end of the decade, recite one Glory Be on the space before the next Our Father bead. Then say the Our Father and announce the next mystery. Repeat in this fashion until you have completed three trips around the rosary's circlet, saying 150 Hail Marys and fifteen Our Fathers, letting the words of the prayers and the images of the mysteries fill your mind. Then return to the medal.

The Fatima Prayer and the Hail Holy Queen Prayer

Upon returning to the medal, many Catholics conclude their rosary session with one of the two following prayers:

The Fatima Prayer

> O my Jesus, forgive us our sins, save us from the fires of hell and lead all souls to heaven, especially those in most need of Thy mercy. Amen.

The Hail Holy Queen Prayer

Hail, Holy Queen, Mother of Mercy, our life, our sweetness, and our hope. To you do we cry, poor banished children of Eve. To you do we send up our sighs, mourning, and weeping in this valley of tears. Turn then, O most gracious advocate, your eyes of mercy toward us and after this our exile show unto us the blessed fruit of your womb, Jesus. O clement! O loving! O sweet Virgin Mary! Pray for us, O Holy Mother of God. That we may be made worthy of the promises of Christ.

Can Protestants Pray the Catholic Rosary?

Garry Wills reminds us that the rosary was developed before the Protestant Reformation, "so that the rosary is part of the history of Protestants as well as Catholics." And several innovative Protestant leaders have, over the years, tried to persuade their flocks to adapt the Catholic rosary for their own use, sometimes changing a few prayers, subtracting a few and adding others. And John Paul II, in his 2002 apostolic letter *The Rosary of the Virgin Mary*, welcomed all Christians to the practice of the rosary, saying that its prayers to the Virgin Mary should be an invitation to remember the son by honoring his mother.

If all of this is true, how did Protestant Christianity fall away from the use of the rosary? According to Wills, the rosary got a black mark from reformers in the Middle Ages when the Catholic Church decided that people could earn an "indulgence" by saying it. Indulgences were papal dispensations from the length of time a soul must spend in purgatory to atone for sins committed during life. Indulgences were a primary cause of the Protestant Reformation, near the top of Martin Luther's Ninety-Five Theses that he nailed to the door of Wittenberg Castle Church in 1517. After Luther broke with the Catholic Church, the rosary remained linked to the tainted practice of indulgences in the minds of the people who eventually became Protestants.

Praying the rosary is no longer a get-out-of-purgatory-free card. And, as Wills says, speeding through the rosary to get the indulgence is not conducive to the spirit of contemplative prayer.

I am a Protestant and I love using the Catholic rosary and regularly incorporate it into my prayer practice. For me, the main attraction is the lovely Hail Mary prayer, which resounds in my core.

The words are taken from two of my favorite scenes in the New Testament. They are my favorites because they are among the happiest scenes in the whole Bible and have women and their domestic concerns at their heart. The first, beginning with "Hail Mary"—*Ave Maria* in the church's Latin—is taken from the greeting of the angel of the Annunciation as he tells Mary she is pregnant (Luke 1:28). The second is based on the words of Elizabeth, as she greets Mary soon after and feels her own baby move inside her: "And Elizabeth was filled with the Holy Spirit and exclaimed with a loud cry, 'Blessed are you among women, and blessed is the fruit of your womb'" (Luke 1:42). Both of these scenes focus on the most feminine of ideas—that of women as nurturers. The last part of the prayer—asking Mary to pray for us sinners—was added in the fifteenth century. In the middle of the prayer—also added in the fifteenth century and forming what John Paul II described as the "center of gravity" of the prayer—is the word "Jesus." It is the fulcrum of the whole prayer, he said—the whole reason for its existence—and should be powerful enough to draw any and all Christians into its heart.

One cannot recite the Rosary without feeling caught up in a clear commitment to advancing peace, especially in the land of Jesus, still so sorely afflicted and so close to the heart of every Christian.

JOHN PAUL II, "THE ROSARY OF THE VIRGIN MARY"

The New Testament scenes on which the Hail Mary prayer is based come just before one of the most glorious of all biblical prayers, the Magnificat of Mary. It is the longest spoken passage attributed to Mary in the Bible and offers its most complete portrait of this remarkable woman. For an exceptionally meaningful session with my Anglican rosary, I combine the Magnificat with the Hail Mary prayer, usually reciting a Hail Mary on the cruciform beads and spreading the Magnificat across the weeks beads (see chapter six).

Praying to Mary in this way is a window into the life of Jesus, allowing us, in a sense, to approach the son through the eyes of the mother. In the words of John Paul II:

> Against the background of the words Ave Maria the principal events of the life of Jesus Christ pass before the eyes of the soul. They take shape in the complete series of the joyful, sorrowful, and glorious mysteries, and they put us in living communion with Jesus through—we might say—the heart of his Mother. At the same time our heart can embrace in the decades of the Rosary all the events that make up the lives of individuals, families, nations, the Church, and all mankind. Our personal concerns and those of our neighbor, especially those who are closest to us, who are dearest to us. Thus the simple prayer of the Rosary marks the rhythm of human life.

Without contemplation, the rosary is a body without a soul.

POPE PAUL VI—DITTO

Though it's a deeply beautiful form of prayer, the Catholic rosary may not match the rhythms of your life and spirituality. But other rosaries have been developed that tap into the heart and depth of praying with beads. In fact, the Anglican or Protestant rosary was developed out of just such a desire to use a form of prayer beads while honoring the Protestant faith of its first users.

An Anglican Rosary with no cross.

CHAPTER THREE

THE ANGLICAN ROSARY

Without prayer the Christian life, robbed of its
sweetness and beauty, becomes cold and formal,
and dead; but in the secret place where God talks
with his own, the Christian life grows into such
a testimony of Divine power that all men will feel
its influence and be touched by the warmth of its
love. . . . That, surely is the purpose of all real
prayer and the end of all true service.

—E. M. BOUNDS, *PURPOSE IN PRAYER*

The Anglican rosary has much in common with other prayer beads. Like
the mala, the subha, and the Catholic rosary, it is circular. Like the earlier forms
of prayer beads, it also has a strand of beads extending from the main circle.
Like almost all prayer beads, it is intended not to be worn, but to be held in the
hands and passed through the fingers. But unlike its predecessors, it has a format and symbolism that is distinctly Protestant.

The true aim of prayer is to enter into conversation with God. It is not restricted to certain hours of the day. A Christian has to feel himself personally in the presence of God. The goal of prayer is precisely to be with God always.

GEORGES FLOROVSKY

The Creation of the Anglican Rosary

The Anglican rosary evolved in the early 1980s from a contemplative prayer group drawn from an Episcopal congregation in Cedar Hill, Texas. For a number of years, members of the Church of the Good Shepherd and their pastor, the Rev. Lynn C. Bauman, had an ongoing group that explored various prayer traditions. They spent time studying *lectio divina*, centering prayer, chanting, body prayer, and other contemplative practices. Eventually, they took up the Catholic rosary, learning the prayers and praying them as a group. It wasn't long before they wanted to move beyond those prayers to something more experimental, but Bauman was uncomfortable with tampering with the centuries-old Catholic tradition. "My gut level feeling was that the Catholic rosary should be left intact," Bauman told me. "I just thought we should respect its use and not experiment with it. We had used various prayer forms of other religious traditions, but we kept them within their world and we felt we should do the same for the Catholic form." So he decided his group would make their own original rosary.

Bauman meditated on what kind of prayer beads and prayers would be suitable for his group, which was composed not just of Episcopalians, but of people from a variety of Christian backgrounds. He had traveled to other countries and was familiar with the Orthodox prayer rope, the Islamic subhah, and the Hindu and Buddhist malas. But the idea of tampering with those seemed wrong, too. What he really wanted was something that was emblematic of his group's common Christian foundation.

To begin the new rosary, Bauman looked for something that would draw from both the Eastern and Western branches of Christianity, forming a bridge between both. He decided on a San Damiano cross, which has a second bar across its top and bears an icon of the crucified Jesus surrounded by his disciples. This cross was originally brought to Italy by Serbian monks, and is now closely associated with Saint Francis of Assisi, forming a link to the Catholic Church to which the humble Italian saint belonged.

Next, he decided on an invitatory bead as the first bead above the cross. Bauman likens the purpose of this bead to that of the prayer of invitation in the Daily Office in The Book of Common Prayer, the book of liturgies, services, and prayers used by members of the churches of the Anglican Communion worldwide. The purpose of this bead, Bauman said, is to invite God's presence, to ask God to draw near as we pray.

After the invitatory bead, the circle, or path, of the rosary begins. For this, Bauman chose thirty-two beads—four groups of seven beads each, separated by four larger beads, one between each set of seven. These numbers are not random, but have many layers of Christian symbolism, something Bauman was eager to infuse into this new rosary. In the Judeo-Christian tradition, seven is the number of perfection and is most closely associated with God. In Genesis, it was on the seventh day that God rested. It is also the number of church sacraments—baptism, confirmation, communion, ordination, marriage, confession, and the anointing of the sick—and the number of seasons in the church calendar—Advent, Christmas, Epiphany, Lent, Holy Week, Easter, and Pentecost. Bauman also wanted this new rosary to be used every day, and there are seven days in a week. For that reason, he named these four groups of beads "the weeks." "It was a way of thinking through the wonder of prayer—that our days of the week should be days of prayer," Bauman said.

Four, the total number of larger beads on the circle of the rosary, is significant, too: there are four times for prayer in the Episcopal prayer book (morning, noonday, evening, and compline). It is also the number of the seasons of the solar year (winter, spring, summer, and fall) and the peaks of the lunar

Real prayer comes not from gritting our teeth but from falling in love

RICHARD FOSTER

A season of silence is the best preparation for speech with God.

Samuel Chadwick

year (the spring and fall equinoxes and the summer and winter solstices). There are four elements (earth, wind, water, and fire) and four cardinal directions (north, south, east, and west). There are four cardinal virtues (prudence, justice, fortitude, and temperance), which form the foundation of Christian life, and four Gospels (Matthew, Mark, Luke, and John), that support the structure of that foundation.

But the greater significance became apparent when Bauman joined all thirty-two beads in a circle—the four larger beads formed a cross, the ultimate symbol of Christianity. It was natural, then, to call these "the cruciform beads."

By entering the circle formed by the weeks and cruciform beads, Bauman says, the person who prays the Anglican rosary is drawn into one of the great mysteries of Christian life. "Through birth each of us has entered the wheel and in time we are called pilgrims," he writes in *The Anglican Rosary*. "Our spiritual journey through the temporal realm, by way of the cross, is the central purpose of our existence in this world. One means of that journey is, of course, through prayer, and prayer moving around the time's wheel represented in the structure of the [Anglican] Rosary symbolizes our spiritual journey following Christ as Lord and Master."

Jesus is memorialized in the total number of beads—thirty-three—the number of years he is believed to have lived among us. This was an unintentional outcome of Bauman's design, but one he was deeply moved by. It also formed another link to the Eastern branch of Christianity, as when one prays the Anglican rosary the recommended three times around, the total number of prayers equals one hundred (ninety-nine prayers on the beads and one on the cross)—the same number of knots on many Eastern Orthodox prayer ropes.

From the beginning, Bauman wanted this new Anglican rosary to be more free-form and experimental than the Catholic rosary, so he did not compose a single set of prayers for the new beads, but instead encouraged users to find and write their own. "What we discovered in our contemplative prayer group is that as we grow our needs change and so do our expressions of prayer and faith," he said. "So there is a need to allow something to evolve with us. That evolution of spirit is crucial, and sometimes you may need prayers that are less complex—maybe one word and a whole lot of silence. We wanted people to be able to have that."

When Bauman took the new Anglican rosary to his contemplative prayer group, it was an immediate hit. They first applied chants and Scripture passages to the new beads, as well as selections from The Book of Common Prayer and prayers from other religious traditions. The new practice spread as members showed their Anglican rosaries to friends and members of other churches, and Bauman soon found himself teaching other groups how to make and use it. Today, though he is no longer an Episcopal priest, he still keeps an Anglican rosary made from stone beads in his pocket. Praxis for Prayer, the contemplative community he directs in Telephone, Texas, still makes and sells Anglican rosaries to people of various faith backgrounds around the world. "It is still very much a part of my life," he said.

The Mechanics of the Anglican Rosary

Each of the thirty-three beads and the cross of the Anglican Rosary is assigned its own prayers. Between these are a number of spacer beads, which are uncounted and have no prayers, but serve to carry our fingers from one counted bead to the next. We will look at specific prayers for all these beads in the second section of the book.

The value of a man resides in what he gives and not in what he is capable of receiving.

ALBERT EINSTEIN

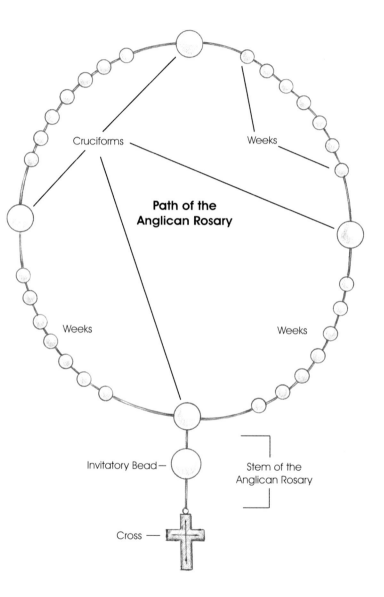

Cruciforms

Weeks

Path of the Anglican Rosary

Weeks

Weeks

Invitatory Bead—

Stem of the Anglican Rosary

Cross —

The Cross

To begin, grasp the cross or charm with your dominant hand. If you are comfortable making the sign of the cross, you may want to make it here, either before you begin the first prayer, or as you recite it. You can touch the rosary's cross to your head, heart, and left and right shoulders to you make this sign.

On the cross, we want to invoke the name of God in all his forms, so prayers that invoke the Trinity are often used here. Or you may start with the Lord's Prayer or any other prayer that is special to you. When you are done, let your fingers slip over the spacer beads and grasp the invitatory bead.

The Invitatory Bead

This is the bead that invites us into the sacred circle of the rosary. This bead functions like the Request for Presence prayer in the Daily Office, asking God to be with us as we pray. You may also want to say the Apostles' Creed here (see page 21), either as you begin the rosary or as you exit it or both, if you like. The Lord's Prayer is also a good prayer for this bead.

The Cruciform Beads

Move over the spacers to the first cruciform bead, the entry into the main circle of the rosary. There are four cruciform beads, representing the four arms of the cross. The prayers said on them should be a bit special, perhaps a statement of what you are praying for—comfort, praise, thanksgiving, healing, peace, and so on.

The Weeks Beads

Now you are in the heart of the rosary, well on the path of prayer. Your fingers should continue to move over the spacer beads, grasping the larger weeks beads

Prayer is the Christian life, reduced to its essence.

Hank Hanegraaff

as you recite the main prayers of the rosary. You may recite one prayer twenty-eight times, fourteen times, or seven times—the choice is yours and God will hear you whatever you do. At times, you may want the simplicity of one phrase repeated twenty-eight times. At others, you may welcome twenty-eight different phrases—perhaps the verses of an entire psalm, canticle, or poem. Again, the choice is yours.

Exiting the Rosary

When you have completed a circuit of the twenty-eight weeks beads, you will find yourself back at the first cruciform bead. Skip over this bead (you already recited it when you entered the main path of the rosary) and return to the invitatory bead. Here you can repeat the Lord's Prayer or recite something else—perhaps the Apostles' Creed or a prayer that sums up your intentions. Then come back to the cross or charm and repeat its prayer, or another one you like. If you feel comfortable with it, you may, as Catholics sometimes do, kiss the cross before you put your rosary away.

You can pray the Anglican rosary once, twice, or three times around. I recommend three times. The trip around the rosary doesn't take long enough for me to become immersed in the contemplative heart of my prayer time, so I need more time with my beads. Three times around can take up to fifteen or more minutes, depending on your choice of prayers—a reasonable time to sit quietly in prayer and meditation.

The principle exercise which the children of God have is to pray. For in this way they give true proof of their faith.

JOHN CALVIN

Other Forms of Prayer Beads

It isn't only Anglicans who are rediscovering this ancient prayer tool. Today, members of several mainline Protestant denominations, including Lutherans, Presbyterians, and Methodists, are taking up the Catholic rosary and other prayer beads, or crafting their own rosary forms and prayers.

Some Lutherans believe that Martin Luther was not opposed to the rosary and its recitation, but only to its overuse and, especially to the granting of the indulgences associated with it. Though not officially adopted by the Evangelical Lutheran Church in America nor the Lutheran Church-Missouri Synod, some Lutherans have compiled a set of prayers for recitation on the traditional Catholic rosary. This form of the rosary also involves meditating on sets of mysteries, and many of the prayers are the same, or nearly so. For example, both Lutherans and Catholics recite the Lord's Prayer on the Our Father beads, but Lutherans add the final line recited by most Protestants, "For thine is the kingdom, and the power, and the glory forever and ever. Amen." They also recite the doxology in the spaces before the Our Father beads—the same prayer that Catholics know as the Glory Be.

But there are some significant differences. On the crucifix, instead of the Apostles' Creed, Lutherans invoke the Trinity: "In the name of the Father, and of the Son, and of the Holy Spirit. Amen." And on the three Hail Mary beads of the stem, and on all of the decades beads, Lutherans say the Jesus Prayer: "Lord Jesus Christ, Son of God, have mercy on me, a sinner." And when Lutherans have completed the decades and return to the medal, they do not say the Hail Holy Queen or the Fatima Prayer, but recite the first half of the traditional Hail Mary prayer: "Hail Mary, full of grace, the Lord is with thee. Blessed art thou among women and blessed is the fruit of thy womb, Jesus." They may also use the medal to pray The Magnificat of Mary, or a prayer called "Evangelical Praise of the Mother God":

> O blessed virgin, Mother of God, what great comfort God has shown us in you, by so graciously regarding your unworthiness and low estate. This encourages us to believe that henceforth He will not despise us poor and lowly ones, but graciously regard us also, according to your example. Amen.

They then return to the crucifix and repeat the invocation of the Trinity.

There is another Lutheran rosary crafted by the Evangelical Lutheran Church in America and sanctioned for use as a Lenten practice. The stem of the rosary has a cross followed by three small beads and a larger fourth bead. On the cross, one invokes the Trinity, praying "God the Father, Son, and Holy Spirit watch over me. Amen." The first bead is for the Apostles' Creed, the second is for the Lord's Prayer, and the third is for a prayer of Martin Luther's:

> I give thanks to you, my heavenly Father through Jesus Christ your dear Son, that you have protected me this night from all harm and danger, and I ask you that you would also protect me today from every sin and all evil, so that my life and actions may please you completely. For into your hands I commend myself: my body, my soul, and all that is mine. Let your holy angel be with me, so that the wicked foe may have no power over me. Amen.

The fourth bead is called the Ash Wednesday bead, and it has no set prayer, but it is suggested that one pray for one's sinfulness and ask for renewal. Likewise, there are no set prayers for the circlet of this rosary, which has forty-two beads. These beads are divided into six groups of seven—one for each Lenten weekday, represented with smaller beads, and one for each Lenten Sunday, represented with larger beads. At the end of the circle is one even larger "Easter bead." The church's website has a full description of suggested petitions and meditations for each bead at www.elca.org/communication/rosary.html.

"The Pearls of Life" is another Lutheran rosary created by Martin Lonnebo, a Swedish pastor. In his book about the Pearls, Lonnebo writes that he developed this form of the rosary when he was emerged in a longing for silence and found himself randomly drawing pictures of a rosary. His design has eighteen beads, or pearls, with twelve round ones and six oblong ones. Each pearl has a different meaning, with the largest gold pearl representing God. The beads are:

- The round gold "God bead" reminds us that God is always with us and loves us.

- Six oblong "Pearls of Silence" remind us to shut out our distractions and that as we approach God, words are not necessary

- The small white "I Pearl" reminds us to turn inward and that we are created in God's image.

- The larger white "Baptism Pearl" shows us we can start over.

- The beige "Desert Pearl" represents hardness and difficulties that cause us to sharpen our focus.

- The blue "Serenity Pearl" represents faith and courage in the color of sky and water.

- Two red "Love Pearls," one for being loved and one for loving others.

- Three small white "Mystery Beads" stand for our inner secrets.

- The black "Night Pearl" represents darkness and doubt.

- The white "Resurrection Pearl" stands for faith and hope that triumph over all.

If I should neglect prayer but a single day, I should lose a great deal of the fire of faith.

Martin Luther

Lonnebo named his rosary *Frälsarkransen*, Swedish for "the wreath of Christ." It, too, has no assigned prayers, but leaves supplicants free to pray whatever they please.

"The Ecumenical Miracle Rosary" was developed in the 1990s by Dennis Di Mauro, a Lutheran married to a Catholic. He had seen his wife and others pray the rosary and wanted a similar devotional practice that was more in line with his Protestant faith. In 1999, he posted his version of the rosary on the Internet. It involves the use of a Catholic rosary, but employs some different prayers. The Nicene Creed takes the place of the Apostles' Creed on the crucifix, and a prayer called "The Greatest Commandment" is said on the three Hail Mary beads of the stem and on all of the decades beads:

> Sweet Jesus, I love you with all my heart and all my soul. Help me to serve my family and everyone else I meet today.

Where Catholics would say a Glory Be, Di Mauro has inserted a prayer called "The Great Commission":

> Oh my lord, I know that you are always with me. Help me to obey your commandments and lead me to share my faith with others, so that they may know and love you.

Upon returning to the medal at the end of the rosary, Di Mauro suggests reciting the Jesus Prayer: "Lord, Jesus Christ, have mercy on me, a sinner." And during the entire recitation, users of this rosary meditate on sets of Jesus' miracles instead of on the traditional Catholic mysteries. Di Mauro hopes to unite peoples of many faiths through the use of this rosary, and often organizes worldwide recitations over the Internet and through telephone link-ups. A more detailed description of this rosary can be found at www.ecumenicalrosary.org.

As it is the business of tailors to make clothes, and the business of cobblers to mend shoes, so it is the business of Christians to pray!

MARTIN LUTHER

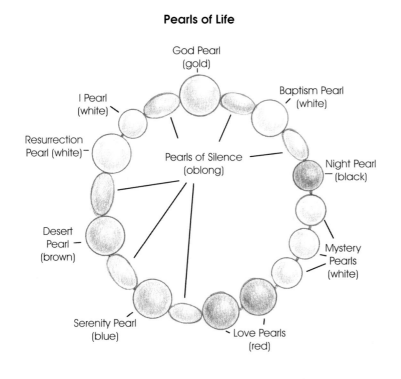

Pearls of Life

God Pearl (gold)

Baptism Pearl (white)

I Pearl (white)

Resurrection Pearl (white)

Pearls of Silence (oblong)

Night Pearl (black)

Desert Pearl (brown)

Mystery Pearls (white)

Serenity Pearl (blue)

Love Pearls (red)

Now that we know the different types of rosaries, we can explore some of the techniques used to pray with them. Some of these techniques will be easy to pick up. Others will require more effort, practice, and especially patience. But with a little perseverance, the pathway to meaningful prayer with beads will open wide.

Some Anglican Rosaries.

CHAPTER FOUR
PRAYING WITH PRAYER BEADS

God is a circle whose center is everywhere
and circumference nowhere.

—Voltaire

To pray with any set of prayer beads is to embark on a journey. It will be a journey full of paradoxes and contradictions. We will be traveling by ourselves, but on it we will never be alone. We will be going somewhere, but we will sit almost entirely still. It will be a journey of words conducted in total or near silence. We will travel far, but go only in circles. When we return, we will have gone away without ever having left where we are.

Learning the steps of this journey is the easy part—those are the beads themselves. But staying on those steps is harder: we need the tools of focus, attention, and purpose to help us say the prayers that go with the beads. And by no means are these tools exclusive to any one form of prayer beads. They are the foundation of any meaningful religious practice, Christian or otherwise. Because of that, the principles of contemplation and prayer sketched here can be applied to all prayer beads—an Anglican or a Catholic rosary, a mala or subhah, or some form you may invent for yourself. The number and configuration of the beads is not what is important. It is the intention behind them—the desire to draw nearer to God—that is crucial.

Praying with *In*tention and *At*tention

Prayer beads are a contemplative prayer tool. The word "contemplation" has its roots in Latin and Greek meaning "to look at things" and "in the temple." Contemplation as a spiritual practice dates back at least to the Middle Ages to a book called *The Cloud of Unknowing* by an anonymous English monk who advises his student to seek God not through knowledge, but through love. Saint Teresa of Avila and Saint John of the Cross, two Christian mystics, later defined contemplative prayer as kind of supernatural state in which the intellect and the will are suspended. Instead, the mind enters a state of *knowing* ("looking" in the roots of the word) instead of a state of *doing*. These two saints, experts at contemplative prayer, described intense feelings of love for God and an almost physical sense of God's presence in their lives. In the mid-1950s, Thomas Merton, a Trappist monk, helped revive contemplation for modern Christians by describing his own practice in many books and articles. Thomas Keating, another Trappist monk, gave a spark to contemplative prayer, which he calls centering prayer, in his 1986 book, *Open Mind, Open Heart*. "Contemplative prayer is the opening of mind and heart—our whole being—to God, the Ultimate Mystery, beyond thoughts, words and emotions," Keating writes. "We open our awareness to God whom we know by faith is within us, closer than breathing, closer than choosing—closer than consciousness itself."

I pray—for fashion's word is out

And prayer comes round again—

That I may seem, though I die old

A foolish, passionate man.

W. B. Yeats

Learning to pray contemplatively takes practice, but there are a few simple things that can help. First, sit in a quiet place: a church sanctuary, your backyard, a secluded corner of a park or beach, a bedroom. Even a bathtub will do if that's the only place you can be alone and undisturbed in your home. You may want to sit before a visual aid—an icon or a picture or painting that induces in you a peaceful state. Sit still for a few minutes in silence. Try to narrow the circle of your attention only to your breath. Breathe in and out slowly a few times, lowering your heart rate and calming your body. Spend a few minutes in quiet reflection, and when you feel calm and still, pick up your prayer beads and begin praying.

Don't *think* about what you're praying for—it's better not to think at all when you pray—but *focus* on what you are praying for. If your prayer is for peace, keep the *idea* of peace before you. Keep the *feeling* of peace within you as you pray. Contemplate it, using your heart, not your head. Thinking will take you out of the mysterious realm of prayer and back into the all-too concrete world of daily obligations and demands.

That's easy to say and hard to do. This is where intention and attention come into play. In the New Testament, Jesus tells us to beware of vain repetitions of prayer. He's not warning against the repetition of prayer— if he were, we would need to say the Lord's Prayer only once, like a pledge. The key word is *vain*. Jesus is warning against becoming disconnected from our prayers to the point that we are just repeating a series of words without meaning, like a mantra intended to induce a meditative state. Rather, our prayers said on beads should be deeply felt statements of faith, of praise, of joy that we keep emotionally attached to *at all times during the praying*. This is to pray with *intention*.

What about *attention*? This is where the tactile nature of the beads comes in. The physical act of grasping a bead, of rotating it gently between the fin-

God is the infinite intellectual sphere with as many circumferences as centers and whose center is everywhere and circumference nowhere. He is entire in his least part.

MEISTER ECKHART

gers, of *feeling* it, will anchor you to the words of the prayer attached to the beads. As you pray, really feel each bead. How hard is it? Is it round or oval? Faceted or smooth? Cool or warm to the touch? Let the feel of the beads ground you in the prayer. If you feel your mind wandering, squeeze or hold the bead tighter. Your attention will come back to the presence of God.

Directing your breathing will also help; this is a well-known and widely practiced method for contemplative prayer. As you begin each prayer, breathe in on the first half and out on the second half. This is a technique tailor-made for prayer beads because the prayers assigned each bead are usually fairly short. For example, if you are praying the Jesus Prayer ("Lord Jesus Christ, have mercy on me."), inhale on "Lord Jesus Christ" and exhale on "have mercy on me."

Remember that contemplative prayer takes practice. Be patient with yourself. It is hard to turn off the buzz of everyday life, with all its demands, and with the increasing connectedness modern technology forces on us. Your time with your prayer beads is a time to put aside these distractions—cell phones, e-mail, schedules, and so on—and be with the simplest essence faith can be reduced to: a reaching outward and upward toward the divine.

Memorizing or Reading Prayers?

Some people find it preferable to memorize prayer, but it's a matter of taste and convenience. You may like repeating the prayers without having to refer to a book or a printed card, but it may not always be possible for you to do so. When I walk my dog, for instance, I can't carry along a book or piece of paper to consult. But I do have one hand free for my beads, which I carry in my pocket. This is when I recite the Jesus Prayer, or the 23rd Psalm, long ago com-

Pray as you can for prayer doesn't consist of thinking a great deal, but of loving a great deal."

St. Teresa of Avila

mitted to memory, or some other simple prayer. At other times, I get out a journal in which I keep all the prayers I like to use with my beads. Keeping a journal like this enables me to take my gathered prayers with me when I travel. My journal is also where I remind myself of the prayers I love and where I keep track of insights that come to me in the midst of my prayer bead sessions. It is part journal, part diary, part notebook, and I keep it by the side of my bed at all times.

Some Things to Remember

Although there are no hard and fast rules for praying with prayer beads, a few guidelines are helpful and may enrich your experience.

First, prayer beads are a *tool for prayer* and not an *object of devotion*. The prayers said with the aid of any prayer beads are always more important than the beads with which they are numbered. You don't need beads to pray. They are not there to *be* the focus of your prayers, but to *help* you focus your prayers. So if you find yourself more concerned with the color of your prayer beads than the content of your prayers, you may want to think about why you are using prayer beads.

Second, don't spend too much time and energy worrying about getting the words of the prayers right—the words are secondary to their intention, which is to draw close to God. Because of this, the words do not have to be articulated in a way that would make a Shakespearean actor jealous. Nor do they have to be recited with 100 percent accuracy. They are stepping-stones to God, and if you forget one or two or leap over a couple here and there, it will not matter—as long as you keep your attention and intention in sight.

The holier a man is, the more does he estimate prayer; the clearer does he see that God gives himself to the praying ones, and that the measure of God's revelation to the soul is the measure of the soul's longing, importunate prayer for God.

E. M. BOUNDS

❧

Those are the basics of praying with prayer beads, and they can be applied to any of their many forms. But as the Anglican rosary is more free-form than its Catholic cousin, there are whole landscapes of prayer that can be arranged—and rearranged—to suit it. In the next section, we will explore some of these prayers, putting into practice what we have learned about rosaries and other prayer beads.

PART TWO

PRAYERS OF FAITH

Two Anglican Rosaries.

CHAPTER FIVE
CREATING PRAYERS FOR THE ANGLICAN ROSARY

Do not try to find exactly the right words for your prayer:
how many times does the simple and monotonous stuttering
of children draw the attention of their father!

—JOHN CLIMACUS, SIXTH CENTURY MYSTIC

Now that you know your way around the Catholic and the Anglican rosaries, you will want to give them a try. The prayers for the Catholic rosary are outlined and explained in chapter two, and I suggest you try them. Then, if you like, you can assign them different prayers of your own choosing. But the Anglican rosary has no prescribed prayers. In the twenty-five years since this rosary appeared, people have compiled and composed many prayers for it. Many of these prayers can be found on Internet sites dedicated to the Anglican rosary, and I have included some of them in chapter seven. Lynn Bauman, the Anglican rosary's creator, includes many prayers he favors in his booklet *The Anglican Rosary*.

But don't forget that you're free to create your own prayers for the Anglican rosary—or any other prayer beads—borrowing from the many prayer resources available—prayer books, liturgies, poems, hymns and songs, and the Scriptures themselves. You can also write your own prayers, giving voice to the inner longing of the soul as it seeks something greater than itself. And you may also apply any of these prayers to other forms of prayer beads by adding or subtracting a few repetitions or by mixing and matching to suit your needs. The prayers assigned here to the Anglican rosary's cross will work for the Catholic rosary's crucifix; the invitatory bead's prayers can be said on the Hail Mary beads; the cruciform prayers can be recited in place of the Our Fathers; and the weeks beads prayers will suit the decades beads by adding three repetitions.

Using the Works of Others

One important thing to remember—the work of contemporary writers is copyrighted. If you are looking for material for your own private and personal use, that's fine. But if you plan to share the prayers you adapt with your friends or your prayer group, you must get permission from the writer or publisher, and you must give the writers credit for their work. Most publishers can be found on the Internet and permission can usually be gained by e-mailing or writing to them.

But there is so much material in the public domain I have only rarely had to seek permission to include someone's writing in this book. A piece of writing is in the public domain when it is no longer protected by a copyright, either because the original copyright expired, the author has been dead for more

Be awake and pray.

Matthew 26:41
and Mark 13:33

than seventy years, or the author has, for some reason, failed to fulfill the necessary steps to regain the copyright after its original expiration. It can then be used by anyone without permission from anyone. According to U.S. federal law, anything written *before* 1923 is currently in the public domain. Anything published between 1923 and 1963 is copyrighted for twenty-eight years and is in the public domain if no one renewed the copyright in the twenty-eighth year. For anything else that you'd like to print in a service flyer or otherwise distribute, seek permission.

Praying the Psalms

This may be the richest treasure trove of prayers for prayer beads. The composers of these poems cover all the emotions of spiritual expression—praise, suffering, joy, sorrow, peace. Look through them, read them aloud, take pieces from several of them and compile your own. On the Anglican rosary, I find they work best for the weeks beads—some are so charged with feeling that reciting seven lines of a psalm four times over the four sets of weeks is more than enough to express myself to God. Others are so beautiful I want to say the whole psalm on all twenty-eight weeks beads. For the rest of the beads, I pick and choose as the mood takes me. When I exit the rosary, returning to the invitatory bead and the cross for the third time, I say the Lord's Prayer and the Apostles' Creed. Here is a set of prayers I use most often, especially at times when I feel overwhelmed. The cruciform prayer is from Psalm 42, the invitatory prayer is from Psalm 19, and the weeks prayers are from Psalm 69. You can refer to the original in your Bible or prayer book to compare my version to the original.

On the Cross

Glory to the Father, to the Son, and to the Holy Spirit.
As it was in the beginning is now and will be forever. Amen.

On the Invitatory Bead

Let the words of my mouth and the meditation of my heart be acceptable
in your sight,
O Lord, my strength and my redeemer.

On the Cruciform Beads

As the deer longs for the water-brooks,
So my soul longs for you, O God.

On the Weeks Beads

1. Save me, O God, for the waters have risen up to my neck.
2. I am sinking in deep mire, and there is no firm ground for my feet.
3. I have come into deep waters, and the torrent washes over me.
4. O God, you know my foolishness, and my faults are not hidden from you.
5. But as for me, this is my prayer to you.
6. In your great mercy, O God, answer me with your unfailing help.
7. Answer me, O Lord, for your love is kind; in your great compassion, turn to me.

Here is another set of prayers for the weeks beads, from Psalm 23. Most people don't use the language of old King James anymore, but for me, this psalm is not the same without its poetry—the language provides an unbroken thread from me back through time to the Christians who prayed on the first rosaries. For the rest of the beads, I use the same prayers in the above set.

On the Weeks Beads

1. The LORD is my shepherd, I shall not want.
2. He maketh me to lie down in green pastures: he leadeth me beside the still waters.
3. He restoreth my soul: he leadeth me in the paths of righteousness for his name's sake.
4. Yea, though I walk through the valley of the shadow of death, I will fear no evil:
5. for thou art with me; thy rod and thy staff they comfort me.
6. Thou preparest a table before me in the presence of mine enemies: thou annointest my head with oil; my cup runneth over.
7. Surely goodness and mercy shall follow me all the days of my life: and I will dwell in the house of the LORD forever.

Here is one adapted from Psalm 25, a song in praise of God. Adapted to the Anglican rosary, it is a joyous declaration of faith, worthy of daily repetition.

On the Cross

Glory to the Father and to the Son and to the Holy Spirit.
As it was in the beginning is now and will be for ever. Amen

On the Invitatory Bead

To you, O Lord, I lift up my soul;
My God, I put my trust in you.

It is not enough to say prayers, one must become, be prayer, prayer incarnate. It is not enough to have moments of praise. All of life, each act, every gesture, even the smile of the human face, must become a hymn of adoration, an offering, a prayer. One should offer not what one has, but what one is.

PAUL EVDOKIMOV,
RUSSIAN ORTHODOX
THEOLOGIAN

On the Cruciform Beads

Show me your ways, O Lord, and teach me your path.

On the Weeks Beads

1. Lead me in your truth, and teach me, for you are the God of my salvation.
2. Remember, O Lord, your compassion and love, for they are from everlasting.
3. Remember not the sins of my youth and my transgressions; remember me according to your love and for the sake of your goodness, O Lord.
4. Gracious and upright is the Lord; therefore he teaches sinners in his way.
5. He guides the humble in doing right and teaches his ways to the lowly.
6. All the paths of the Lord are love and faithfulness to those who keep his covenant and his testimonies.
7. My eyes are ever looking to the Lord, for he shall pluck my feet out of the net.

There are more psalms that are easily adapted to the Anglican rosary than I can list here. Chapter seven is a collection of prayers from various sources, including the Psalms, to mix and match on the Anglican rosary, or other prayer beads, as it suits your needs or moods.

Prayers from Poems

Poets of every nation and religion have wrangled with the relationship between God and human beings, using words to describe what is, for most of us, indescribable. Many have succeeded in capturing the essence of our longing for

God. One of the best at this was Christina Rossetti, a nineteenth-century fervent Christian and a member of the Church of England. She was passionate in her love for God and gifted in her ability to put that love on the page. This is one of her poems:

A Better Resurrection

I have no wit, no words, no tears;
My heart within me like a stone
Is numbed too much for hopes or fears.
Look right, look left, I dwell alone;
I lift mine eyes, but dimmed with grief
No everlasting hills I see;
My life is in the falling leaf:
O Jesus, quicken me.
My life is like a faded leaf,
My harvest dwindled to a husk:
Truly my life is void and brief
And tedious in the barren dusk;
My life is like a frozen thing,
No bud nor greenness can I see:
Yet rise it shall—the sap of spring;
O Jesus, rise in me.
My life is like a broken bowl,
A broken bowl that cannot hold
One drop of water for my soul
Or cordial in the searching cold;
Cast in the fire the perished thing;
Melt and remold it, till it be

Man is fond of counting his troubles, but he does not count his joys. If he counted them up as he ought to, he would see that every lot has enough happiness provided for it.

FYODOR DOSTOEVSKY

A royal cup for Him, my King:
O Jesus, drink of me.

To turn this into a prayer for the Anglican rosary is simple. Each stanza of the poem has eight lines—seven for the weeks beads and one for the adjacent cruciform bead. Conveniently, the last lines of each stanza are repetitive and related to each other and, in fact, form a kind of trinity of pleas to Jesus. I like to begin my prayer beads with the Lord's Prayer, so I'll say that as I hold the cross. For the invitatory bead, I could use a collect from The Book of Common Prayer, but I discovered a prayer written by Rossetti in an anthology, which seems to fit beautifully here. As for the one remaining cruciform bead, I will repeat the line of her poem that most resonated with me. Here is the result:

On the Cross

The Lord's Prayer

On the Invitatory Bead

Teach us, O Lord, to fear you without being afraid, to fear you in love that we may love you without fear.

On the First Cruciform Bead

O Jesus, rise in me.

On the First Set of Weeks Beads

1. I have no wit, no words, no tears;
2. My heart within me like a stone
3. Is numbed too much for hopes or fears.

All you need to do to learn to pray is to pray.

WESLEY DUEWEL

4. Look right, look left, I dwell alone;

5. I lift mine eyes, but dimmed with grief

6. No everlasting hills I see;

7. My life is in the falling leaf.

On the Second Cruciform Bead

O Jesus, quicken me.

On the Second Set of Weeks Beads

1. My life is like a faded leaf,

2. My harvest dwindled to a husk:

3. Truly my life is void and brief

4. And tedious in the barren dusk;

5. My life is like a frozen thing,

6. No bud nor greenness can I see:

7. Yet rise it shall—the sap of spring.

On the Third Cruciform Bead

O Jesus, rise in me.

On the Third Set of Weeks Bead

1. My life is like a broken bowl,

2. A broken bowl that cannot hold

3. One drop of water for my soul

4. Or cordial in the searching cold;

5. Cast in the fire the perished thing;

6. Melt and remold it, till it be

7. A royal cup for Him, my King.

On the Fourth Cruciform Bead

O Jesus, drink of me.

On the Fourth Set of Weeks Beads

Repeat the prayers for the first set of weeks.

Who are some of your favorite poets? Are there poems you memorized in school? Browse a poetry anthology for other prayers that you can pray with the Anglican rosary or other prayer beads.

Prayers from Hymns and Songs

In American musical theater, characters break out in song when the spoken word is not enough to carry the emotion and the impact of what they need to say. Think of *West Side Story*'s Tony and Maria on the fire escape singing, "Tonight, tonight, there's only you tonight / What you are, what you do, what you say." It's similar with hymns. The best hymns are prayers that are so heavy with emotion, so important to lift up that they must be sung instead of merely spoken. Thought of this way, the lyrics of hymns can make lovely prayers for reciting with an Anglican rosary.

I find that traditional hymns—those written before 1950, let's say—work best for me. The language of the lyrics tends to be more poetic, more rarified, more like a prayer to me. I also like the idea that in praying the lyrics of a hymn I am connecting myself to the unknown thousands of people who have sung this song throughout the ages—people who worshipped in white clapboard New England churches, people who were sent out as missionaries, people who lived long ago, perhaps, but were just like me in their yearning toward God.

You may prefer something more contemporary. There is only one rule: if the words of the song speak to you, then use them.

I more easily reach a place of prayerful contemplation with the lyrics to hymns I do not know the music to. That way, while I am reciting the words with my beads, I am not also hearing the melody in my head, which can be distracting.

But having said that, here's an example of an old hymn, *Be Thou My Vision*, which I have sung in church since childhood and know very well. Its words lovingly cry out for the closeness of God. In its rejection of material reality for the ultimate reality of God, I hear echoes of Julian of Norwich's prayer, "God of your goodness, give me yourself, for you are enough for me." Here are the lyrics, based on an old Irish folksong, arranged by Eleanor H. Hull in the latter half of the nineteenth century.

Be Thou My Vision

Be thou my Vision, O Lord of my heart;
Naught be all else to me, save that thou art;
Thou my best thought, by day or by night,
Waking or sleeping, thy presence my light.

Be thou my Wisdom, and thou my true Word;
I ever with thee, and thou with me, Lord;
Thou my great Father, and I thy true son,
Thou in me dwelling, and I with thee one.

Riches I heed not, nor man's empty praise;
Thou mine inheritance, now and always;
Thou and thou only, first in my heart,
High King of heaven, my treasure thou art.

God does nothing but in answer to prayer.

JOHN WESLEY

High King of heaven, my victory won,
May I reach heaven's joys, O bright heaven's Sun!
Heart of my own heart, whatever befall,
Still be my Vision, O Ruler of all. Amen.

For the Anglican rosary, I make some adjustments. First, I toss out the anti-quated language. This breaks up the rhyme scheme and helps to ban the melody, as lovely as it is, from my mind while I pray. Also, I keep only the first two verses, the ones that mean the most to me, and I take a couple of lines from the last verse to say on the cruciform beads. For the cross I invoke the Holy Trinity, and for the invitatory bead I take a verse from Psalm 98 that describes the joy of singing to God. The result looks like this:

On the Cross

In the name of the Father, the Son, and the Holy Spirit,
As it was in the beginning is now and will be forever. Amen.

On the Invitatory Bead

Shout with joy to the Lord, all you lands;
Lift up your voice, rejoice and sing.

On the Cruciform Beads

High King of heaven, you are my treasure. You, and only you, are first
   in my heart.

On the Weeks Beads

1. Be my vision, O Lord of my heart.
2. Nothing means anything to me, save what you are.

Meditation is the tongue of the soul and the language of our spirit.

JEREMY TAYLOR

3. You are my best thought, by day or by night.
4. Waking or sleeping, your presence is my light.
5. Be my Wisdom and my true Word
6. I ever am with you and you with me, Lord
7. You are my great Father, and I your true child.

Look through your church hymnal or through other songbooks to find more hymns that can be prayed on the Anglican rosary or other prayer beads.

Prayers from Prayer Books and Anthologies

People of every faith tradition have been writing prayers for millennia, and there are shelves full of books that collect them. In chapter eleven, I have compiled a list of some of these books that I've found most helpful. Among my favorites of these sources is *Women's Uncommon Prayer: Our Lives Revealed, Nurtured, Celebrated*, a compilation of the prayers of contemporary Episcopal women. It includes the prayers of every kind of woman I can think of—mothers and children, clergy and seekers, professionals and housewives and many more. The prayers are deeply felt, truly original, and cover every circumstance where faith plays a role—birth, death, marriage, illness, abuse, barrenness, aging, the loss of a child, and the death of a pet. Here is one of these prayers:

For Making Me a Woman

by Marty Conner

For making me a woman
in what still so often
seems a man's world,
I thank you.

Because you taught me by example
that power is your gift,
and not my possession.

For giving me a body
though it sometimes fails me
and is not all I wish it was
or rather, a good deal more
than I wish it was,
I thank you.
Because you taught me
that I am much more
than my body
and yet my body is
your holy temple.

For calling me to be
more than I believe I can be,
and less
than I sometimes pretend I am,
I thank you.
Because you taught me
that being is more than doing,
that who I am
and whose I am
are more important than
what I do
or what I have.

For all that you are
Creator,
Redeemer,
Sanctifier,
Great "I Am,"
I bless you
as you have so greatly blessed me.

And here, with a little help from Psalm 25 for the Invitatory bead, is how I adapted it to the Anglican rosary:

On the Cross

The Lord's Prayer

On the Invitatory Bead

To you, O Lord, I lift up my soul;
My God, I put my trust in you.

On the Cruciform Beads

For all that you are, Creator, Redeemer, Sanctifier, Great "I Am,"
I bless you as you have so greatly blessed me.

On the Weeks Beads

1. For making me a woman in what still so often seems a man's world,
   I thank you.
2. Because you taught me by example that power is your gift, and not
   my possession.

O, Lord, may the mantle of silence become a cloak of understanding to warm our hearts in prayer.

KATE MCILHAGGA

3. For giving me a body though it sometimes fails me and is not all I wish it was, I thank you.
4. Because you taught me that I am much more than my body and yet my body is your holy temple.
5. For calling me to be more than I believe I can be, and less than I sometimes pretend I am, I thank you.
6. Because you taught me that being is more than doing
7. That who I am and whose I am are more important than what I do or what I have.

Collections of prayers, both contemporary and traditional, are legion. Your library and local bookstore will offer you a start. Ask your pastor where he or she turns when in need of a prayer.

Giving Voice to Your Own Prayers

You do not need to use the words of others on your prayer beads. You can write your own. These do not have to be complicated prayers, worthy of a psalmist. They are not going to compete in a poetry contest or fall under the eyes of a strict editor before being published. They are for you and God alone. So how to write them? Read the quote from John Climacus, a sixth-century monk, which appears at the beginning of this chapter: "Do not try to find exactly the

We would not have any think that the value of their prayers is to be measured by the clock, but our purpose is to impress on our minds the necessity of being much alone with God; and that if this feature has not been produced by our faith, then our faith is of a feeble and surface type.

E. M. Bounds

right words for your prayer," he wrote to a brother. "How many times does the simple and monotonous stuttering of children draw the attention of their father!" God does not care what words we use in prayer, only that we are in prayer. There is no one—not even yourself—that you need to impress with your literary gifts. Just listen to your heart and let the words come out. Again, this underscores the great beauty of prayer beads as a prayer tool—there is no right, there is no wrong. There is only prayer.

Beads and Crosses.

CHAPTER SIX
PRAYING THE ANGLICAN ROSARY WITH THE SAINTS

The brethren asked Abba Agathon, "Amongst all our different activities, Father, which is the virtue that requires the greatest effort?" He answered, "Forgive me, but I think there is no effort greater than praying to God. For every time a man wants to pray, his enemies, the demons, try to prevent him; for they know that nothing obstructs them so much as prayer to God. In everything else that a man undertakes, if he perseveres, he will attain rest. But in order to pray, a man must struggle to his last breath."

—*THE SAYINGS OF THE DESERT FATHERS*, SIXTH CENTURY CE

We can also glean prayers for the Anglican rosary and other prayer beads by sifting through the writings of some of the great men and women of God—sages, monks, nuns, theologians, pastors, priests, missionaries, and activists—who were powerful warriors of prayer. These people can teach us how to pray through their example, and adapting their words to the use of prayer beads can take us deep into the heart of the contemplative prayer tradition.

Praying with Mary

As a woman, I often want to pray with words written by or attributed to another woman who has gone before me. Who better to pray with than the mother of God? The following is taken from Luke 1:38 and the The Magnificat, or Song of Mary (Luke 1:46–55). Mary speaks these words just before and after the Angel of the Annunciation delivers the news that she, a virgin, is expecting a child. You know the story. I like to pray these words on my prayer beads because of what it can teach us about finding God's blessings in the challenges that come our way.

On the Cross

> Glory to the Father, and to the Son, and to the Holy Spirit;
> As it was in the beginning, is now and will be for ever. Amen.

On the Invitatory Bead

> Here am I, the servant of the Lord, let it be with me according to your will.

On the Cruciform Beads

> My soul proclaims the greatness of the Lord,
> My spirit rejoices in God my Savior.

On the Weeks Beads

> 1. He has mercy on those who fear him in every generation.
> 2. He has shown the strength of his arm.
> 3. He has scattered the proud in their conceit.

4. He has cast down the mighty from their thrones, and has lifted up the mighty.
5. He has filled the hungry with good things, and the rich he has sent away empty.
6. He has come to the help of his servant Israel, for he has remembered his promise of mercy.
7. The promise he made to our fathers, to Abraham and his children for ever.

Praying with Jesus

It is fitting that we should pray the words of Jesus on prayer beads because it was he who taught us to pray when he gave us the Lord's Prayer. Other words of his are so powerful, so weighted with good sense and truth that there is a blessing in reminding ourselves of them in daily prayer. Below are several prayers drawn from the Sermon on the Mount as it is recounted in Matthew 5–7. The first set is taken from the Beatitudes and the second is drawn from Jesus' admonitions to the faithful. You can say one set of these on all the weeks, repeating them four times, or you can alternate between the two, saying each set twice. And as always, feel free to substitute other words of Jesus that may be more meaningful to you.

On the Cross

In the name of the living God, Father, Son, and Holy Spirit.

On the Invitatory Bead

The Lord's Prayer

Prayer is the gate through which all the graces of God come to us.

Teresa of Avila

Prayer fastens the soul to God, making it one with his will through the deep inward working of the Holy Spirit.

Julian of Norwich, *Revelations of Divine Love*

On the Cruciform Beads

> Everyone then who hears these words of mine and acts on them will be like a wise man who built his house on rock. And everyone who hears these words of mine and does not act on them will be like a foolish man who built his house on sand.

On the First Set of Weeks

1. Blessed are the poor in spirit, for theirs is the kingdom of heaven.
2. Blessed are those who mourn, for they will be comforted.
3. Blessed are the meek, for they will inherit the earth.
4. Blessed are those who hunger and thirst for righteousness, for they will be filled.
5. Blessed are the merciful, for they will receive mercy.
6. Blessed are the pure in heart, for they will see God.
7. Blessed are the peacemakers, for they will be called the children of God.

On the Second Set of Weeks

1. Let your light shine before others, so that they may see your good works and give glory to your Father in heaven.
2. Do not store up for yourselves treasures on earth, but store up for yourselves treasures in heaven, for where your treasure is, there your heart will be also.
3. Strive first for the kingdom of God and his righteousness.
4. Do not worry about tomorrow, for tomorrow will bring worries of its own. Today's trouble is enough for today.
5. Do not judge, so that you may not be judged. For with the judgment you make you will be judged, and the measure you give will be the measure you get.

6. Ask, and it will be given to you; search, and you will find; knock, and the door will be opened for you.

7. In everything do to others as you would have them do to you.

Praying with St. Patrick

Patrick was the scion of a middle-class Roman family of Christians living in fourth-century Britain. When he was just sixteen years old, he was captured by raiders and sold as a slave in Ireland. He tended a flock of sheep on a cold stretch of Irish hillside, alone, hungry, and cold. He did nothing but pray. After six years, he had a vision in which a voice told him to board a ship and go home. But after returning to his family, Patrick was tortured by dreams and visions of Jesus telling him to return to the Irish and bring his word to them. He did, becoming the first missionary after Paul. Patrick was, according to historian Thomas Cahill, the first voice to speak out against slavery, a practice he helped end in Ireland. He also worked to stifle tribal warfare and other forms of accepted violence, and was a champion for the plight of women and the poor. The following prayer, often called "Saint Patrick's Breastplate" because it was thought to have the power to invoke an armorlike protection, is attributed to him. The translation is by Whitley Stokes, John Strachan, and Kuno Meyer. The Anglican and Catholic Churches celebrate St. Patrick on his feast day, March 17.

On the Cross

I bind unto myself today
the strong Name of the Trinity,
by invocation of the same,
the Three in One, and One in Three.

On the Invitatory Bead

The Lord's Prayer

On the Cruciform Beads

I bind unto myself the Name,
Of whom all nature hath creation,
eternal Father, Spirit, Word.

On the First Set of Weeks

1. I bind this day to me forever by power of faith, Christ's Incarnation;
2. His baptism in the Jordan river;
3. His death on the cross for my salvation;
4. His bursting from the spiced tomb;
5. His riding up the heavenly way;
6. His coming at the day of doom:
7. I bind unto myself today.

On the Second Set of Weeks

1. I bind unto myself today the virtues of the starlit heaven,
2. The glorious sun's life-giving ray,
3. The whiteness of the moon at even,
4. The flashing of the lightning free,
5. The whirling wind's tempestuous shocks,
6. The stable earth, the deep salt sea,
7. Around the old eternal rocks.

Man has turned his back on silence. Day after day he invents machines and devices that increase noise and distract humanity from the essence of life, contemplation, meditation.

JEAN ARP

On the Third Set of Weeks

1. I bind unto myself today the power of God to hold and lead,
2. His eye to watch, his might to stay,
3. His ear to hearken to my need;
4. The wisdom of my God to teach,
5. His hand to guide, his shield to ward;
6. The word of God to give me speech,
7. His heavenly host to be my guard.

On the Fourth Set of Weeks

1. Christ be with me, Christ within me,
2. Christ behind me, Christ before me,
3. Christ beside me, Christ to win me,
4. Christ to comfort and restore me,
5. Christ beneath me, Christ above me,
6. Christ in quiet, Christ in danger,
7. Christ in hearts of all that love me, friend and stranger.

Praying with Julian of Norwich

Julian was one of the great Christian mystics. She was born in 1342 in Norwich, England. In her thirties, she became very ill and believed she was dying. During her suffering, she had a series of visions—"shewings," in her words—of Christ's passion and of the Virgin Mary. She recovered, and then dedicated herself to a life of contemplation and became the anchorite—a kind of hermit who resides in a church—at the Church of St. Julian in Norwich. It is from the church that we get her name—her true identity is unknown. Julian lived in a small cell with a single window that opened into the sanctuary, and from there she could hear Mass and give spiritual advice to pilgrims. For twenty years, she lived in her cell, meditating upon her visions, finally writing them down in *Revelations of Divine Love*, the first book by a woman to be published in English, in about 1393.

Julian lived in a time of great upheaval. The Black Death swept through Europe several times, killing millions and almost certainly touching Julian's family and neighbors. The Catholic Church was in schism, and the theology of the day was that God was angry with a world of sinners and inflicted these ills as punishment. Yet Julian's most famous saying and prayer was that "all manner of things would be well." In her writings, she described her religious philosophy:

> For a man regards some deeds as well done and some as evil,
> and our Lord does not regard them so,
> for everything which exists in nature is of God's creation,
> so that everything which is done has the property of being God's doing.

For Julian, God was in everything, even the bad things, working to bring about the best end. "God is more nearer to us than our own soul," she wrote. She planted herself not in the darkness, but in the light. For that reason, I find praying her words on prayer beads to be a rallying cry in the darkest of times, a way to trust God to bring peace and love, hope and redemption. The following comes from two sources—the prayer for the cross comes from Julian's poem *I am That*, an invocation of the Trinity, and the rest comes from her *Revelations of Divine Love*. The Catholic Church marks her feast day on May 13 and both the Anglican Church and the Evangelical Lutheran Church in America remember her on May 8.

On the Cross

> I am that which is highest,
> I am that which is lowest,
> I am that which is All.

On the Invitatory Bead

> The Lord's Prayer

On the Cruciform Beads

> God of your goodness, give me yourself
> For you are enough for me.
> I cannot properly ask anything less to be worthy of you.
> If I were to ask less, I should always be in want
> For only in you have I all.

On the Weeks Beads (on Every Bead)

> All shall be well and all shall be well,
> And all manner of thing shall be well.

Praying with Saint Francis of Assisi

Born in 1181, Francis was christened John by his mother after John the Baptist, but his father, a wealthy merchant, had the baby rechristened Francesco. No son of his was going to be a man of God, but was going to follow him into the cloth trade.

   As a teenager, Francis liked to party and drink. And like many young men, he had dreams of glory in battle, getting his chance when Assisi declared war

That in order to form a habit of conversing with God continually, and referring all we do to Him; we must at first apply to Him with some diligence: but that after a little care we should find His love inwardly excite us to it without any difficulty.

BROTHER LAWRENCE

on nearby Perugia. Decked out in the finest armor his father's money could buy, Francis went to war. But less than a day from home, he had a dream in which God told him to turn around. He did, to great humiliation. He began to pray and, at one point, kneeling in Assisi's Church of San Damiano, he heard God call him to repair his church. Francis—now in his twenties—renounced his family and his wealth. He slept in the woods, beginning a stewardship of animals and nature that is still associated with him today. He preached a literal interpretation of the gospel—that all creatures are our brothers and we should care for and love them. At his death at the age of forty-five, more than five thousand people had flocked to him, forming what came to be known as the Friars Minor, the Franciscan order. Within the Anglican Communion, his spirit lives on in the Society of Saint Francis, an order of men and women who take vows of chastity, poverty, and obedience.

The prayer most associated with Saint Francis begins, "O, Lord, make me an instrument of your peace." Yet it is certain that Saint Francis did not write this prayer, as the first record of its appearance is in a French magazine in 1912. In the United States, it became widely known in 1936 when Cardinal Francis Spellman, Archbishop of New York, championed its use. Regardless of its origin, it remains one of the most heartfelt appeals for a useful, meaningful existence in the service of others.

In 1226, as Saint Francis lay dying, he sang Psalm 141: "O Lord, I call to you; come to me quickly; hear my voice when I cry to you." I have incorporated that into the following. You may say the prayer below as it is written, or repeat only the section for the first set of weeks beads throughout. The prayer for the cross comes from Francis's *The Praises of the Trinity*. His feast day is celebrated in the Catholic Church and the Anglican Church on October 4.

True, whole prayer is nothing but love.

ST. AUGUSTINE

On the Cross

> Holy, holy holy, Lord God almighty,
> Who is and who was and who is to come.
> Let us praise and exalt him above all for ever.

On the Invitatory Bead

> The Lord's Prayer

On the Cruciform Beads

> O Lord, I call to you; come to me quickly; hear my voice when I cry to you.

On the First and Third Set of Weeks

1. Lord, make me an instrument of your peace,
2. Where there is hatred, let me sow love;
3. where there is injury, pardon;
4. where there is doubt, faith;
5. where there is despair, hope;
6. where there is darkness, light;
7. where there is sadness, joy.

On the Second and Fourth Set of Weeks

1. O Divine Master, grant that I may not so much seek to be consoled as to console;
2. to be understood as to understand;
3. to be loved as to love.
4. For it is in giving that we receive;

5. it is in pardoning that we are pardoned;
6. and it is in dying that we are born to eternal life.
7. Amen.

Francis is also known for a poem he wrote in 1224, *Canticum Fratris Solis*, or *The Canticle to Brother Sun*. Since the 1960s, this has become an anthem of the environmental movement, currently gaining strength throughout the Christian community. When I pray with my prayer beads out of doors—on the beach, on a hike in the woods or hills, or just in the sunshine of my backyard—the words of Saint Francis ground me in the beauty of creation and open my eyes to seeing God in a leaf of a tree, a grain of sand, and the warmth of the sun.

On the Cross

Holy, holy holy, Lord God almighty,
Who is and who was and who is to come.
Let us praise and exhalt him above all for ever.

On the Invitatory Bead

Most high, all powerful, all good Lord! All praise is yours, all glory, all honor, and all blessing.

On the Cruciform Beads

Be praised, my Lord, through all your creatures.

On the Weeks Beads

1. Be praised, my Lord, through Brother Sun, who brings the day; and you give light through him. And he is beautiful and radiant in all his splendor! Of you, Most High, he bears the likeness.

2. Be praised, my Lord, through Sister Moon and the stars; in the heavens you have made them, precious and beautiful.

3. Be praised, my Lord, through Brothers Wind and Air, and clouds and storms, and all the weather, through which you give your creatures sustenance.

4. Be praised, My Lord, through Sister Water; she is very useful, and humble, and precious, and pure.

5. Be praised, my Lord, through Brother Fire, through whom you brighten the night. He is beautiful and cheerful, and powerful and strong.

6. Be praised, my Lord, through our sister Earth, who feeds us and rules us, and produces various fruits with colored flowers and herbs.

7. Be praised, my Lord, through those who forgive for love of you; through those who endure sickness and trial. Happy those who endure in peace, for by you, Most High, they will be crowned.

Praying with Saint Thomas Aquinas

Thomas was born a nobleman in Italy in 1225. Against the wishes of his family, he became a Dominican priest. He is best known for his work *Summa Theologia*, a detailed summary of his religious philosophy that is still studied today. Thomas believed that we should petition God often for gifts and virtues through prayer. Among the virtues he thought were worth asking for were the cardinal virtues: prudence, temperance, justice, and fortitude. He also defined the three theological virtues: faith, hope, and charity. Thomas died in 1274, the greatest theologian the Catholic Church has ever known. I have arranged two sets of rosary prayers from Saint Thomas's own prayers. The first set is taken

If we know the divine art of contemplation, easily and consciously we can unite the inner world and the outer world.

SRI CHINMOY

from Aquinas's advice for structuring a meaningful life. When reciting this, I meditate on one of the four cardinal virtues on each of the sets of weeks beads, asking God to give me a greater helping of them. The second set, taken from a writing of Aquinas's called *Before Study*, is just for the weeks beads. Combine it with the cross, invitatory, and weeks beads prayers of the first set. It is a very centering and settling prayer to say before beginning any task. Both the Catholic Church and the Anglican Church celebrate his feast day on January 28.

For Ordering a Life Wisely

On the Cross

> The Lord's Prayer

On the Invitatory Bead

> Grant me, O Lord my God, a mind to know you, a heart to seek you, wisdom to find you,
> conduct pleasing to you, faithful perseverance in waiting for you, and a hope of finally embracing you.

On the Cruciform Beads

> Put my life in good order, O my God
> Grant that I may know what you require me to do.

On the First Set of Weeks

> 1. O Lord my God, make me, submissive without protest
> 2. Poor without discouragement,
> 3. Chaste without regret,
> 4. Patient without complaint,

5. Humble without posturing,

6. Cheerful without frivolity,

7. Mature without gloom.

On the Second Set of Weeks

1. O Lord my God,

2. Let me fear you without losing hope,

3. Be truthful without guile,

4. Do good works without presumption,

5. Rebuke my neighbor without haughtiness,

6. Strengthen him by word and example without hypocrisy,

7. And bring to perfect completion whatever is pleasing to you.

On the Third Set of Weeks

1. Grant unto me, my God, that I may direct my heart to you.

2. Give to me a watchful heart.

3. Give to me a noble heart.

4. Give to me a resolute heart.

5. Give to me a stalwart heart.

6. Give to me a temperate heart.

7. Give to me a loving heart.

On the Fourth Set of Weeks

1. Give to me, O Lord my God,

2. Understanding of you,

3. Diligence in seeking you,

4. Wisdom in finding you,

Never for any reason whatever neglect to pray.

St. Teresa of Avila

5. Discourse ever pleasing to you,
6. Perseverance in waiting for you,
7. And confidence in finally embracing you.

Before Study

On the Weeks Beads

1. Ineffable Creator, grant me keenness of mind,
2. Capacity to remember,
3. Skill in learning,
4. Subtlety to interpret,
5. And eloquence in speech.
6. May you guide the beginning of my work,
7. Direct its progress, and bring it to completion.

Praying with Dietrich Bonhoeffer

Dietrich Bonhoeffer was a German Lutheran pastor who protested against the Nazi persecution of the Jews. He was involved in a plot to assassinate Hitler, which led to his arrest and execution by hanging in 1945. He is considered a martyr by many denominations, including the churches of the Anglican Communion. The following is drawn from two sources, his *Prayer in Time of Distress* and *Prayers from Prison*. I come to this prayer only in times of great pain or stress and always come away from it with a sense that others, like Bonhoeffer, have gone before me into great darkness and found their way out. It is also a prayer of great comfort because it promises God will give us no more than we can handle.

I saw that He is all that is good as to my understanding. And in this He showed me a little thing the size of a hazel nut lying in the palm of my hand it seemed. And it was round as any ball. I looked on it with my understanding and I thought what may this be. And it was answered generally thus, "It is all that is made."

JULIAN OF NORWICH,
*REVELATIONS
OF DIVINE LOVE*

On the Cross

O, heavenly Father, I praise and thank you.

On the Invitatory Bead

You have granted me many blessings;
Now let me also accept what is hard from your hand.
You will lay on me no more than I can bear.

On the Cruciform Beads

O God, early in the morning I cry to you.
Help me to pray and to concentrate my thoughts on you:
I cannot do this alone.

On the Weeks Beads

1. In me there is darkness, but with you there is light;
2. I am lonely, but you do not leave me;
3. I am feeble in heart, but with you there is help;
4. I am restless, but with you there is peace.
5. In me there is bitterness, but with you there is patience;
6. I do not understand your ways, but you know the way for me.
7. Lord, whatever this day may bring, your name be praised.

These are just some of the people whose words have leapt out to me in my times of prayerful need. Again, in keeping with the essence of the free-form nature of most prayer beads, feel free to mix and match them, delete some, and incorporate others into your prayer time. Who else might we pray with on our prayer beads? Whom do you admire for their achievements, their strength, their will, their thoughts and deeds for others?

Two Anglican rosaries.

CHAPTER SEVEN

PRAYING IN OUR JOYS AND SORROWS

Although God certainly knows all our needs, praying for them changes our attitude from complaint to praise and enables us to participate in God's personal plan for our lives.

—RAY STEDMAN, *TALKING WITH MY FATHER*

*F*or all of us, there are times when the events in our lives draw us to God in prayer for healing, strength, and discernment. Here are some prayers I have found suitable for those times in my own life. I have adapted these prayers primarily for the Anglican rosary because it is the form of Christian prayer beads with no standard set of prayers. But again, you may also pray these prayers on the Catholic rosary by making a few adjustments. Prayers said on the cross of the Anglican rosary can be said on the Catholic rosary's crucifix, and prayers for the Anglican rosary's invitatory bead can be said once on each of the three Hail Mary beads on the Catholic rosary's stem. Likewise, prayers for the Anglican rosary's four cruciform beads can be repeated an additional three times to fit the Catholic rosary's sets of ten decades beads. If you are praying with a set of Pearls of Life, you are even less restricted. Its eighteen beads have no set prayers, so you may choose any you like, mixing and matching as you see fit.

And while I have assigned these prayers to specific beads, these assignments are, for the most part, random, and some prayers will work on more than one type of bead. So just as you should feel free to organize these prayers as you like, you can also feel free to pray them on different beads. What you pray is between you and God, who will hear you regardless of what bead you are holding and what words you are saying. I have also rearranged some of the pronouns, changing the plural to the singular and the second person to the first, to make the prayers more personal and immediate. Feel free to change them again.

Prayers for the Stem of the Rosary

Prayers for the Cross or Crucifix

Holy God, Holy and Mighty, Holy and Immortal, have mercy on us.
(Liturgy of Saint John of Chrysostom)

Almighty God, you have poured upon us the new light of your incarnate Word: Grant that this light, enkindled in our hearts, may shine forth in our lives; through Jesus Christ our Lord, who lives and reigns with you, in the unity of the Holy Spirit one God, now and for ever.
(The Book of Common Prayer)

At least—to pray—
is left—is left—

Oh Jesus—
in the Air—

I know not which
thy chamber is—

I'm knocking—
everywhere—

EMILY DICKINSON

O God the Father, creator of heaven and earth,
O God the Son, redeemer of the world,
O God, the Holy Ghost, sanctifier of the faithful,
O holy, blessed, and glorious Trinity, one God,
Have mercy on me.

> (The Book of Common Prayer)

Before you, Father, in righteousness and humility,
With you, Brother, in faith and courage,
In you, Spirit, in stillness.

> (prayer of Dag Hammarskjöld)

The hands of the Father uphold me,
The hands of the Savior enfold me,
The hands of Spirit surround me.

> (David Adam, *The Edge of Glory*)

God the Sender, send me.
God the Sent, come with me.
God the Strengthener of those who go, empower me,
That I may go with you and find those who will call you
    Father, Son, and Holy Spirit.

> (Welsh prayer, source unknown)

May God the Father bless us,
May Christ take care of us,
May the Holy Ghost enlighten us all the days of our life.

> (prayer of Saint Ethelwold)

Prayers for the Invitatory or Three Hail Mary Beads

This is the day the Lord has made. Let us rejoice and be glad in it.
(Psalm 118:24)

Come, Holy Spirit, fill the hearts of your faithful and kindle in them
 the fire of your love.
Send forth your Spirit and they shall be created,
And you shall renew the face of the earth.
(*The Glenstal Book of Prayer*)

Stir up your power, O Lord, and with great might come among us.
(The Book of Common Prayer)

Give us grace, O Lord, to answer readily the call of our Savior Jesus Christ
 and proclaim to all people the Good News of his salvation.
(The Book of Common Prayer)

Gracious Father, whose blessed Son Jesus Christ came down from heaven
 to be the true bread which gives life to the world: Evermore give us this
 bread, that he may live in us and we in him.
(The Book of Common Prayer)

O God, whose Son Jesus is the good shepherd of your people: Grant that
 when we hear his voice we may know him who calls us each by name,
 and follow where he leads.
(The Book of Common Prayer)

Hidden God, ever present to me,
May I now be present to you,
Attentive to your every word,

Attuned to your inspirations,
Alert to your touch.
(Patricia B. Clark, *Women's Uncommon Prayers*)

Come, true light.
Come, life eternal.
Come, hidden mystery.
(Saint Symeon the New Theologian, *Hymns of Divine Love*)

Prayers for the Cruciform or Our Father Beads

Lord, be a bright flame before me,
Be a guiding star above me,
Be a smooth path below me,
Be a kindly shepherd behind me,
Today and for evermore. Amen.
(prayer of Saint Columba)

O my God, I am sorry for all my sins
Because they offend you, who are so good
And with your help I will not sin again.
(*The Glenstal Book of Prayer*)

My Lord, Jesus Christ, may your peace be with me.
In you, O Jesus, true peace,
May I have peace upon peace eternally.
Through you may I come to that peace which surpasses all understanding,
There, where in gladness, I may see you in yourself.
(prayer of Saint Gertrude of Helfta)

*More things are
wrought by prayer*

*Than this world
dreams of.*

ALFRED,
LORD TENNYSON,
THE IDYLLS OF THE KING

Glory be to God who has shown us the light!
Lead me from darkness to light.
Lead me from sadness to joy.
Lead me from death to immortality.
Glory be to God who has shown us the light!
(*The Glenstal Book of Prayer*)

Into your hands, O Lord, I commend my spirit;
For you have redeemed me, O Lord, O God of truth.
Keep me, O Lord, as the apple of your eye;
Hide me under the shadow of your wings.
(The Book of Common Prayer)

Deep peace of the running water to me,
Deep peace of the flowing air to me,
Deep peace of the quiet earth to me,
Deep peace of the shining stars to me,
Deep peace of the Son of Peace to me.
(Celtic Blessing, source unknown)

Prayers for the Weeks or Decades Beads

The Lord is my light and my salvation; whom then shall I fear?
The Lord is the stronghold of my life; of whom shall I be afraid?
(Ps. 27:1)

God is my refuge and my strength, a very present help in trouble.
(Ps. 46:1)

Prayer is the first thing, the second thing, the third thing necessary to a minister. Pray, then, my dear brother: pray, pray, pray.

EDWARD PAYSON

Have mercy on me, O God, according to your steadfast love.

(Ps. 51:1)

Here am I, the servant of the Lord; let it be with me according to your word.

(Luke 1:38)

O God, be all my love, all my hope, all my striving;
Let my thoughts and words flow from you, my daily life be in you, and
  every breath I take be for you.

(prayer of John Cassian)

O merciful Lord Jesus, forget not me, as I have forgotten thee.

(prayer of Christina Rossetti)

Lord Jesus Christ, your light shines within me.
Let not my doubts nor my darkness speak to me.

(prayer of the Taizé Community)

Lord Jesus Christ, your light shines within me.
Let my heart always welcome your love.

(prayer of the Taizé Community)

Bless the Lord, my soul, and bless God's holy name.
Bless the Lord my soul, who leads me into life.

(prayer of the Taizé Community)

God to enfold me, God to surround me,
God in my speaking, God in my thinking.

God in my sleeping, God in my waking,
God in my watching, God in my hoping.

God in my life, God in my lips,
God in my soul, God in my heart.

God in my sufficing, God in my slumber,
God in mine ever-living soul, God in mine eternity.
(*Carmina Gadelica*, Vols. I and III)

Prayers for the Path of the Rosary

A Prayer for Healing

(Adapted from The Book of Common Prayer)

On the Cruciform or Our Father Beads

O God, the source of all health: So fill my heart with faith in your love, that with calm expectancy I may make room for your power to possess me, and gracefully accept your healing; through Jesus Christ our Lord. Amen.

On the Weeks or Decades Beads

1. Lord Jesus Christ, by your patience in suffering you hallowed earthly pain and gave us the example of obedience to your Father's will:
2. Be near me in my time of weakness and pain;
3. Sustain me by your grace, that my strength and courage may not fail;
4. Heal me according to your will;
5. Help me always to believe that what happens to me here is of little account if you hold me in eternal life,
6. My Lord and my God.
7. Amen.

A Prayer for Coping

(Adapted from Reinhold Niebuhr)

On the Cruciform or Our Father Beads

> God grant me the serenity to accept the things I cannot change;
> Courage to change the things I can;
> And wisdom to know the difference.

On the Weeks or Decades Beads

1. Living one day at a time;
2. Enjoying one moment at a time;
3. Accepting hardships as the pathway to peace;
4. Taking, as He did, this sinful world as it is, not as I would have it;
5. Trusting that He will make all things right if I surrender to His Will;
6. That I may be reasonably happy in this life
7. And supremely happy with Him forever in the next.

A Prayer before Beginning Work

(Adapted from The Book of Common Prayer)

On the Cruciform or Our Father Beads

> Almighty God, our heavenly Father, you declare your glory and show
> forth your handiwork in the heavens and the earth.

Prayer fastens the soul to God, making it one with his will through the deep inward working of the Holy Spirit. So he says this, "Pray inwardly, even though you feel no joy in it. For it does good, though you feel nothing, see nothing, yes, even though you think you cannot pray. For when you are dry and empty, sick and weak, your prayers please me, though there be little enough to please you. All believing prayer is precious in my sight."

JULIAN OF NORWICH,
REVELATIONS OF DIVINE LOVE

On the Weeks or Decades Beads

1. Be present with me as I work;
2. Inspire me to do the work you give me with a singleness of heart.
3. Guide me in the work I do, that I may do it not for self alone, but for the common good.
4. Give me pride in what I do, and a just return for my labor.
5. Make me mindful of the rightful aspirations of other workers.
6. Arouse my concern for those who are out of work.
7. Through Jesus Christ our Lord, who lives and reigns with you and the Holy Spirit, one God, for ever and ever.

A Prayer for God's Aid and Courage

(Adapted from *Carmina Gadelica*, vols. I and III)

On the Cruciform or Our Father Beads

God with me lying down,
God with me rising up,
God with me in each ray of light.

On the Weeks or Decades Beads

1. Thou, my soul's Healer, keep me at even,
2. Keep me at morning,
3. Keep me at noon,
4. On rough course faring,
5. Help and safeguard my means this night.
6. I am tired, astray, and stumbling,
7. Shield thou me from snare and sin.

Prayer is the highest achievement of which the human person is capable.

St. Teresa Benedicta of the Cross

A Prayer for God's Gifts

(Adapted from Saint Bonaventura)

On the Cruciform or Our Father Beads

> Lord Jesus, as God's Spirit came down and rested upon you,
> May the Spirit rest upon me, bestowing his sevenfold gifts.

On the Weeks or Decades Beads

1. First, grant me the gift of understanding, by which your precepts may enlighten my mind.
2. Second, grant me counsel, by which I may follow in your footsteps on the path of righteousness.
3. Third, grant me courage, by which I may ward off the enemy's attacks.
4. Fourth, grant me knowledge, by which I can distinguish good from evil.
5. Fifth, grant me piety, by which I may acquire a compassionate heart.
6. Sixth, grant me fear, by which I may draw back from evil and submit to what is good.
7. Seventh, grant me wisdom, that I may taste fully the life-giving sweetness of your love.

A Prayer for Self-Dedication

(Adapted from Saint Ignatius of Loyola)

On the Cruciform or Our Father Beads

> Lord, Jesus Christ, fill me, I pray with your light and life.

On the Weeks or Decades Beads

1. Dearest Lord, teach me to be generous.
2. Teach me to serve you as you deserve.
3. To give and not to count the cost.
4. To fight and not to heed the wounds.
5. To toil and not to seek for rest.
6. To labor and not to ask for any reward.
7. Save that of knowing that I do your will.

Gold cannot be pure, and people cannot be perfect.

CHINESE PROVERB

PART THREE

BEADS OF FAITH

Rosary beads.

CHAPTER EIGHT
CHOOSING THE RIGHT BEADS

I learned that you should feel when writing,
not like Lord Byron on a mountain top, but like a child
stringing beads in kindergarten—happy, absorbed
and quietly putting one bead on after another.

—BRENDA UELAND, *IF YOU WANT TO WRITE*

One of the beauties of making prayer beads is that they can be made from almost anything—glass or plastic, clay or wood, shell or bone, seeds or ceramic. So how do you go about choosing the right material for your own strand? Because prayer beads are such a personal item, slipping through your fingers in time and in tune with your innermost prayers and thoughts, there are some questions you may find helpful in guiding you to the right materials for your own strand.

What Colors Have Meaning for Me and Will Lead Me to a State of Prayer?

Different colors inspire different and specific feelings in people. For example, I always feel calmed by ocean colors—the blue and green of the water, the beige and white of the sands. The color scheme of my house is entirely ocean-oriented—boring perhaps, but it makes a soothing working and living space for me. So when I make prayer beads, half the time I choose aquas, teals, ambers, tans, bottle greens, and pearly whites. But I have a friend for whom everything must be red, red, red. I love red, but the color makes me feel excited, jumpy, expectant—not, for me, a prayerful attitude. So ask yourself what colors make you feel most attuned to relaxation, reflection, and prayer and choose your beads accordingly.

What Bead Materials Speak Most to Me?

Beads can be made from just about anything you can poke a hole in, opening a world of possibilities for prayer bead makers. But just as there are colors that are more meaningful to each of us, some materials will have more meaning, too. When I make prayer beads, I like to use glass and stone. I love the coolness of the glass beads when I first pick them up, and I like the way they warm up in my hands as I move through the prayers. To me, this mirrors the progression of my mind through my prayer time, starting off a bit detached, but, with repetition, heating up. Crystal, too, is especially meaningful to me for prayer beads. It seems harder and more colorful than regular glass. It refracts light, breaking it into its component parts. With my prayer beads, I want my prayers to refract the meaning and yearning in my heart. Stones are solid and enduring—the way I like to think of myself. Think about the various materials described in the section that follows and ask yourself which best reflects the goals you have set for your prayer time. What has a special parallel with your own life? Is it the sturdy protection a seashell represents? The colorful ceramic glaze on an otherwise plain clay bead? The blend of two weaker metals it takes to make a stronger bronze bead? Perhaps you will see connections between materials and your own situation that no one else can see. Those will be the right beads for you.

My chinaberry beads made by my own hand and strung on a raveling string, or my oakball beads were as satisfying to me as the finest string of pearls.

Velma Ann
Rogers Tower,
Oklahoma pioneer

What Kind of Charm Do I Want at the End of My Prayer Beads?

For many people, the answer is plain: a rosary is not a rosary unless it has a cross at the end. There are plenty of beautiful crosses available, made from all kinds of materials. I have made many sets of rosaries with crosses, and I regularly pray with them. But I also like to make and use rosaries that have a charm that is a less literal symbol of my faith than a cross. I have one set with a beautiful pewter tree, which, for me, is a symbol of the interconnectedness of all things made by God. I have another with a gorgeous piece of irregularly cut pink glass, which reminds me that though God did not make me perfect, I was

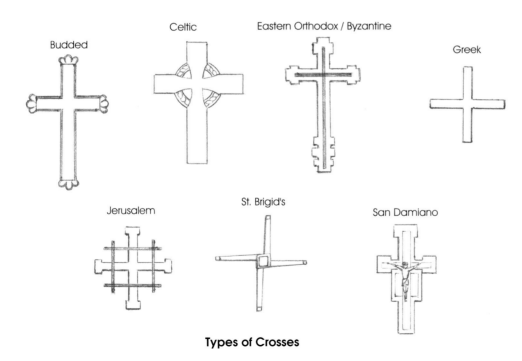

Types of Crosses

made to last. And I have another with a piece of intricately cut jade that reminds me of the complex pattern of my life and the world we inhabit. To me, because God created all things and is in all things, it's fine to put these things at the end of my prayer beads. If this is something you are comfortable with, it can open up a whole new world of possibilities for your prayer beads. Ask yourself if there is anything that symbolizes your faith and feelings about God—a flower? An animal? An image of a saint? A key? A shell? A picture? When you use it, think of it as the emblem of your faith, and say the same prayers on it as you would on a cross or crucifix.

Do I Want My Prayer Beads to Have a Theme?

You could make a set of prayer beads that symbolizes the four elements, with sections of beads devoted by color or material to earth, water, fire, and air. You could make a set that represents your prayers for your family or children, by incorporating their birthstones. You could make a set dedicated to peace by using a peace sign charm. You could make a set for a soldier in red, white, and blue. You could make a set dedicated to the feminine aspect of God, with pastel colors and a feminine-looking charm. *The possibilities are endless.* You just have to put some thought and energy into the meaning behind them.

Choosing Beads

Armed with your answers to these questions, try to find the right beads for you—and others you may want to make prayer beads for—from the many materials beads can be made from.

Glass

There are so many kinds of glass beads: pressed glass beads, lampwork glass beads, fused glass beads, crystal glass beads, millefiore glass beads, furnace glass beads, and fire-polished glass beads, to name just a few of the most popular types. The type of glass bead you use doesn't matter, as long as you like the look of it. My own preference tends toward crystal glass beads, because of the spectacular colors they come in, and for fire-polished glass beads, because of the extra shimmer a trip back into the oven gives them. Among the most popular glass beads today are seed beads, the small round beads that are used in much contemporary bead embroidery and bead-woven jewelry. These come in several sizes, from 15 to 6, with the larger numbers representing the smaller beads. I find that sizes 11 and 8 are good to use as spacers—the small uncounted beads between the larger, counted prayer beads.

Plastic

Of all the materials that beads can be made of, plastic is probably the most versatile and the most durable. It is also among the lightest. For these reasons, plastic beads can make excellent prayer beads for children, travelers, the hospitalized and the sick. And, of course, plastic beads are among the least expensive. You can buy plastic beads at the craft store, but for better quality, go to a bead store. Plastic beads are made in molds and are likely to have a seam. If this will distract you when you pray, a small nail file can be used to buff the seam flush with the rest of the bead.

One seed becomes

An everlasting song,
a singing tree

Jean Toomer,
Song of the Son

*From a small seed
a mighty trunk
may grow.*

AESCHYLUS,
THE LIBATION BEARERS

Shells

A shell is a protective coating made by a delicate sea creature. They are hard and enduring, a sign that something small and insignificant can make something beautiful and lasting. For all these reasons, I love using shells in my prayer beads.

A wonderful plus to using shell beads is that you can collect them yourself and make a strand of prayer beads that is like a string of memories of beaches you loved and good times you shared. All you need is a hand drill or dremel tool with a small drill bit attached to make small holes in your collection. If you don't live near the ocean, many craft and bead stores offer inexpensive strands of shells, complete with holes.

Ivory and Bone

Ivory is made from the teeth of various animals, including elephants, walruses, hippopotamuses, and whales. In 1989, many countries, including the United States, banned the selling of ivory after many African species were nearly wiped out. Don't be afraid to ask bead retailers about the provenance of their ivory beads.

I am very attracted to the warm look and feel of ivory, but feel uncomfortable about using the real thing. Pre-ivory ban or not, I can't get past the fact that some large animal had to die to place it into my hands. Instead, I like a substitution called "vegetable ivory," which is made from the tagua nut from a Central American rainforest palm. It looks like ivory, but no elephants, walruses, whales, or any other animals were harvested for it. Many larger bead stores and online retailers carry tagua. If you must have real ivory, get it from a vintage retailer or other outlet that can prove it was made before the ban.

Native Americans made beads from the bones of animals or from their antlers. Horn takes dye very nicely and can be purchased in a range of colors. Again, though, I am a bit squeamish about using bone if I do not know how it was harvested.

Metal

Metal beads can have good heft, something to consider if you want to feel the weight of your prayer beads as you pray. They may need to be polished, especially with heavy use. Some metal beads are composed of a base metal overlaid with a silver, gold, or copper color. These beads are less expensive than solid silver, copper, or gold beads, but you should be aware that their color will wear off in time.

Gold is a symbol of kings and has been used to adorn religious icons, idols, and images for many thousands of years. In Christianity gold was used in paintings to represent Jesus and the holy family, and in Orthodox Christianity the icons of the many saints are often represented with gold detail or appear on gold backgrounds.

Silver, too, has a long history with religion. In European goddess traditions, silver was closely associated with the moon, the symbol of the feminine aspect of God. Judas, of course, is supposed to have sold Jesus out for thirteen pieces of silver. In the heraldry of the Middle Ages, silver symbolized purity and chastity because it remained unchanged by fire.

Copper was thought by the ancient Egyptians to protect the health of the wearer. Today, some people believe solid copper can battle exhaustion, ease arthritis, and help promote healthy circulation. It has a long association with ancient religions. The ancient Greeks associated copper with the goddess Aphrodite because of its beauty, and Native Americans etched ceremonial and spiritual symbols into copper.

Pewter and bronze are two alloys made of different mixes of tin and copper and sometimes lead. Many beads, spacers, and charms are made from these two metals, which are less expensive than gold and silver, but every bit as durable.

Semiprecious Stones

Naturally occurring semiprecious gemstones have been known since the earliest civilizations and have come to be associated with certain qualities. I like to use them for prayer beads because they are part of the earth, part of its creation story, which has always been a great part of God for me. The Old Testament tells of a bejeweled breastplate worn by Aaron, the high priest of the Hebrews. The armor was set with twelve precious and semiprecious stones—one for each of the twelve tribes of Israel. Among them was amethyst, peridot, onyx, jasper, and agate, all of which are available to beaders today.

There are dozens of these stones, too many to describe in detail here. Instead, let's look at some of the more popular semiprecious stones, most of them available on strands or singly in better bead stores. I use many of these when I make prayer beads for other people, often making strands composed of their birthstones. To find out about gemstones not listed here, consult one of the many excellent books and websites on the subject. I recommend *Cunningham's Encyclopedia of Crystal, Gem, and Metal Magic* by Scott Cunningham as an excellent resource. I mined it for many of the following descriptions.

Agate comes in a range of colors including black, blue, brown, green, and red. Perhaps brown agate, traditionally worn by ancient soldiers to assure victory in battle, was the agate spoken of in Aaron's breastplate. In folklore, agate is the stone of truth, and wearing it is supposed to ensure that one's words are sincere. There are also patterned forms of the stone, such as black and white agate, moss agate, and banded agate.

Amethyst is a quartz that runs in shades from light lavender to deep purple. It has often been associated with royalty because of its color. Different cultures have credited amethyst with numerous qualities and abilities, from symbolizing peace and sincerity to protecting soldiers. In Aaron's breastplate, the amethyst represented the prophet Math, known for his deep desire to please God. Christians of the Middle Ages believed amethyst could promote celibacy and purity, so it was incorporated in many church adornments of the time. In Tibet, amethyst is associated with the Buddha, and many Buddhist prayer beads are made from amethyst. Today, holistic healers believe its contact with the skin can bring about a relaxed state.

Bloodstone, with a dark green base flecked with spots of red, was considered in the Middle Ages to represent the blood of Christ. Sculptures of martyrs made in this period were often carved from bloodstone.

Carnelian is an agate from the chalcedony family. The ancient Egyptians believed carnelian ensured the soul's passage to eternity. The Old Testament lists carnelian as one of the stones in Aaron's breastplate, representing the tribe of Reuben. Those interested in New Age spirituality believe this orange-red stone has great focusing properties and can boost creativity and problem-solving.

Fluorite comes in pretty pastel shades of green, white, purple, and lavender. The ancient Egyptians carved fluorite into scarabs, and the Chinese used it to make decorative and devotional statues. Ancient cultures believed fluorite has an energy that promotes peace and spiritual growth. Contemporary New Age devotees believe it can help distinguish truth from illusion.

Garnets have a rich religious history. One tale holds that Noah used a garnet to light the path of the ark at night. Early Christians associated the garnet with the blood of Christ's sacrifice, and Crusaders wore it in the belief it would help them find their way home. Once, garnets were exchanged as

No seed shall perish which the soul hath sown.

JOHN ADDINGTON SYMONDS

farewell tokens between friends as a symbol of their love for each other and a sign of hope that they would meet again. Muslims believe the garnet illuminates the fourth heaven. Today, garnets are credited with promoting health, order, insight, and strength. Garnets are traditionally the birthstone of January babies.

Jade, to the ancient Chinese, was an emblem of heaven and the earth. Chinese artisans crafted jade Buddhas, altars, and animals as devotional objects. Confucius taught that jade has eleven virtues, including benevolence, fidelity, polite etiquette, wisdom, and sincerity. Hence, jade was not only a decoration, but also a symbol of ethics and good behavior.

Jasper, another of the stones in Aaron's biblical breastplate, is supposed to protect the wearer from physical harm and from pain. Perhaps for this reason, it has a reputation in some folk cultures for reducing the pain of childbirth. In some Native American cultures, jasper was known as the "rainbringer" and was used in religious rituals and ceremonies. Jasper comes in several colors, including red, green, brown, and a mottled variety.

Moonstone is a usually white, milky stone with highlights of lavender and sometimes pink. It was revered by the people of ancient India as sacred, and today it is considered protective of women and children.

Onyx is an agate that comes in green, blue, white, and most commonly black. It is mentioned in the Bible as one of the twelve stones on the breastplate of the high priests, and in Genesis 2:12: "The gold of that land is good; bdellium and the onyx stone are there." In India, onyx was worn to protect against the evil eye, and in the Middle East it was used as a worry stone because people believed it could absorb negative energy.

Pearls have been associated with various goddesses by peoples throughout history. The goddess of the Syrians was known as "the Lady of the Pearls," and

*In this broad
earth of ours,*

*Amid the measureless
grossness and the slag,*

*Enclosed and
safe within its
central heart,*

*Nestles the
seed perfection.*

Walt Whitman,
Song of the Universal

early Saxon religion held that pearls were the tears of the goddess Freya. In ancient Mediterranean cultures, the pearl represented the nurturing aspect of the region's various goddesses. Ancient mystics associated the pearl with God's creation of the universe, as a pearl seemed to be generated out of nothing by the oyster. Today, cultured pearls of all shapes and sizes are readily available in most craft and bead stores.

Peridots were known by the ancient Egyptians as "the jewel of the sun" and by the Hawaiians as "Pele's tears." Other ancient peoples thought they had a great power for healing the sick, and some people still believe that peridots can ease childbirth. They range from a greenish yellow to a deeper olive green and are the birthstone of those born in August.

Sodalite is a dark blue stone with veins of white or yellow. Ancient Egyptians believed it could alleviate fear and bring about a clear mind. Today, some holistic healers believe sodalite can combat the effects of radiation, making this a good choice to give a cancer patient.

Turquoise is associated with the Great Spirit revered by many Native American tribes. The Pueblo Indians of the Southwest placed a piece of the blue and black–veined stone under the floors of their homes as an offering to the gods. The Navajo believed ground turquoise used in sand paintings could bring rain. Most Native Americans of the Southwest revere the turquoise as a protective and healing stone.

Wood

Jesus died on a cross made of wood. For this reason, a rosary made from wood can resonate deeply with Christians. Some legends say the cross was made of dogwood, some say olive, some say cedar of Lebanon. The Bible is silent on this subject, so, for me, any kind of wood bead will do. If you can't find enough wood beads, consider a wooden cross for the end of the rosary. Here are some other kinds of woods that are sacred or special to different religions and cultures.

Sandalwood has a sweet, light scent and is sacred to Hindus, Buddhists, and Zoroastrians. Some ancient Hindu temples in India are built entirely of sandalwood, and many devout Hindus wear a dot of paste made from it on their foreheads. Some Hindus believe sandalwood can bring one closer to the divine, while Buddhists believe the scent of sandalwood can transform one's earthly desires and help in meditation. It is frequently a part of Chinese and Japanese Buddhist worship ceremonies, and Zoroastrians use its branches to sustain their sacred fire.

Cherry. There is an old legend about the Holy Family and a cherry tree. The legend goes that on the way to Bethlehem, Joseph and Mary passed a cherry orchard and Mary, pregnant with Jesus, begged Joseph to pick her some of the fruit. Joseph, out of spite, tells Mary to get the child's real father to pick the cherries for her. At this moment, Jesus speaks from Mary's womb and commands a bough of the cherry tree to come down to her. Joseph witnesses the miracle and repents his harsh words. By the fifteenth century this legend had made its way into a song, known as *The Cherry Tree Carol*. It has been recorded by several artists, including Joan Baez. In the Shinto faith, the wood of the cherry tree is believed to house a divine spirit.

Olive. There are olive tress in the Garden of Gethsemane, some of which, legend claims, go back to the time of Jesus.

Clay and Ceramic

There are many clay beads on the market for beaders, some more refined than others. Some clay beads are plain, dried earth with no paint or glaze. Ceramic beads are made from clay fired at a high temperature and given a decorative glaze. If you choose clay or ceramic beads, be sure they have a sufficiently thick glaze to stand up to all your fingering.

You can also make your own clay beads from polymer clay, which comes in many lovely colors, including gold, silver, and bronze. This can be a fun project to do with children. All you need is a pasta maker to run the clay through, a toaster oven to bake it in, and good, strong hands to roll out the clay. You may also want to brush a layer of clear glaze on the finished beads to give them a shine. There are many excellent books on crafting beads from polymer clay available at craft stores. Similarly, you can make beads from precious metal clay, a clay that burns away to leave its form in sterling silver behind. Precious metal clay is more expensive than polymer clay and requires a special kiln. There are many good books on this subject, too.

Seeds

Some of the first prayer beads were made from seeds. And while we have many more options today, a seed can be a special symbol of faith for prayer beads. In Matthew 17:20, Jesus gave us the seed as a symbol of faith: "For truly I tell you, if you have faith the size of a mustard seed, you will say to this mountain, 'Move from here to there,' and it will move; and nothing will be impossible for you." Used as a touchstone for prayer, a bead made from a seed can represent all that humans can aspire to become and do. It is a hardy symbol of the potential we all hold within us and ask God to help us bring forth.

Seeds have been collected, dried, and strung by faithful people in virtually every corner of the world. Some of these seeds, and the plants they come from can be found in parks, gardens, nurseries, and even health food stores. You may have prayer beads growing in your own backyard. Here are some seeds that can be used for prayer beads:

Remember that the smallest seed of faith is of more worth than the largest fruit of happiness.

Henry David Thoreau

Juniper (Juniperus osteosperma). Juniper trees grow wild in the American desert in the Southwest. They have tough little seeds—about the size of a cherry pit—that have hard brown shells. Juniper seeds were used widely by the Native American tribes of the Southwest. The Navajo refer to juniper seed beads as "spirit beads" or "ghost beads," and they place them around the necks of children to ward off nightmares and evil spirits.

The juniper berry is the female seed cone, so as seeds, they hold the promise of fertility and new life. In the high desert, juniper trees frequently bear the black scars of lightning strikes, taking into their own sturdy bodies the force of the heavens and bearing up under the pain. So as a prayer bead, the juniper seed can also signify strength, resiliency, perseverance, and fortitude in the face of great trials.

Chinaberry, or Persian lilac (Melia azedarach). In India, people place garlands of chinaberry seeds across their doorways to scare off illness and infection. Some Christian cultures have seen in its five-petaled flower a representation of the five wounds Jesus suffered on the cross. Its tough, melon-shaped seeds are easily pierced with an awl or other sharp-pointed tool.

Job's tears (Coix lacryma-jobi). Job's tears are not a real seed, but caryopses, the fruit of a grass. They go by a number of names, including David's tears, Saint Mary's tears, Christ's tears (*lacryma christi*), and just plain tear drops. Job's tears have been used as beads for millennia. A recently excavated site in western India that dated to 2000 BCE had a bead shop with Job's tears hung on the wall to dry.

In the United States, a Cherokee legend holds that when the tribe was forced from their homeland in the Southeastern part of the country, the bereft people left a trail of tears, and these plants appeared wherever a tear fell. In

Mexico, medicine men of the Tarahumara Indians wear Job's tears for protection against sickness.

It's hard to resist turning Job's tears into beads. For one thing, they make their own holes, as one end opens when the plant drops its seed and another opens when the seed is pulled from the plant. Their pale gray color means they can be easily dyed with wood stains or fast-drying enamel paint.

Rudraksha (Elaeocarpus angustifolius). These may have been the earliest form of prayer beads, first used in India. The plant bears a blue fruit that holds a deeply wrinkled, round, brown marble-sized pit, which is rutted and has five lines. Hindus who worship Shiva revere this as the most sacred seed, believing that the god cried when confronted with the sadness of the world and that one of his tears became the first rudraksha tree. Today, it is still considered a sign of Shiva's compassion.

Mix it up

The symbolism of all these beads can be interpreted in myriad ways. And any material can be turned into prayer beads: buttons, bottle caps, and dried peas could even work! But when I reach for one of my sets of prayer beads, I am reaching for one that particularly reflects my mood, my thoughts, my desires at the moment of my prayers. These are very personal choices, and with a little thought, you will come up with your own "best" materials.

Beads and a medal for a rosary.

CHAPTER NINE
MAKING YOUR OWN ROSARIES

To use beads with a prayer,
Indian or Moslem or Christian,
is to enflesh the words,
make thought tangible.

—MADELEINE L'ENGLE,
THE SUMMER OF THE GREAT-GRANDMOTHER

*M*aking a set of prayer beads is one of the simplest crafts a person can do. At their most basic form, they consist of a handful of beads and a string. That's it. It is the simplicity of their creation that makes them the most democratic of prayer tools—virtually anyone who can thread a needle and tie a knot can make a set. But a word of warning—the ease of creating them can also make them addicting. Once you have made your first set, it will be hard not to make a second, a third, and so on. If you're like me, you'll soon have a strand for every purse, every mood, and almost every pocket! Very likely you will want to make some to give away.

Once someone has left behind the habitual prayers of childhood and has entered into the personal encounter, there is no way back. He must live in the light of God and expose and entrust himself to the light ever more conditionally.

ADRIENNE VON SPEYR,
SWISS MYSTIC

Getting Started: Beads

Whether you choose to make an Anglican rosary, a Catholic rosary or another form of prayer beads, the basic tools and materials you will need are the same. You may also choose to make your own unique and personalized set of prayer beads, with the number, shape, size, and color of beads you decide is right for you. You will still need the same basic tools—just adjust the number of beads in the directions below to suit your original design.

Beads for an Anglican Rosary

For an Anglican rosary, you will need a total of thirty-three beads—one invitatory bead, four cruciform beads, and twenty-eight weeks beads. You will also need some uncounted beads to connect all the other beads to each other. Each of these kinds of beads should be different sizes, so your fingers can tell the type of bead without your eyes needing to see them. I like to choose my beads from largest to smallest based on the number I need of each to construct the rosary—the fewer I need of a certain bead, the larger its size will be, relative to the others. So since I need only one invitatory bead, it will be the largest bead. I need four cruciforms, so they will be smaller than the invitatory bead but larger than the weeks beads. Smallest of all will be the uncounted connector beads. You may further distinguish the types of beads by color. For the end of the Anglican rosary, you will need a cross or another kind of charm.

Beads for a Catholic Rosary

To make a Catholic rosary, you will need fifty-nine beads—fifty for the decades, six for the Our Fathers, and three for the Hail Marys. You will also need some uncounted beads to connect them all together. I like to use the largest beads for the Our Fathers, a medium-sized bead for the Hail Marys, and a smaller bead for the decades. You may also choose to use the same bead for the Hail Mary beads and the decades beads, as many rosary makers do. I use the smallest of all beads as connectors to link them to each other. You will need a crucifix or other charm for the end, and you may want to use a special rosary medal to connect the circle of the rosary to the stem. These medals have three holes, and can be found in most bead stores or through online retailers. Chapter eleven has a list of several retail outlets where they can be found.

Getting Started: Beading Thread

When I use the term "thread" to describe what you string your prayer beads with, I am not speaking of traditional sewing thread. That kind of thread is too fragile for stringing beads that will get quite a bit of handling. Instead, I mean any one of several fibers used by jewelry makers to string beads. You should experiment and see which ones you like best. Here are a few:

Nylon cord. This is good for the beginning beader because it comes on a small card with a needle already threaded. It is also fairly strong and comes in a rainbow of bright and subtle colors.

Silamide. This strong nylon thread is pretwisted and prewaxed, giving it good strength. Still, for making prayer beads, I would use a double strand. It comes on spools in many colors. Silamide will not last forever, but it will last a fair amount of time. It should be used only with beads that do not have sharp edges that can cut it, like crystals.

Fiber and cords. Leather, hemp, jute, linen, or synthetic cords can be used to string beads with large holes or to make a knotted prayer rope. These can be found on spools and precut in packages in beading stores, craft stores, and even in fabric stores.

Braided thread and monofilament. These look a lot like fishing line. They are not pretty on their own, but can be inexpensive and are readily available in craft and even hardware stores. Braided thread, such as Power Pro and Fire Line, come in various strengths and can be used with a needle and can be knotted. These are great threads for making prayer beads if flexible beading wire—my favorite material—is too difficult for the beginning beader.

Flexible beading wire. This is several strands of fine wire wrapped together and covered with a coating and is my preferred material for making prayer beads. Flexible beading wire is especially good for prayer beads because it comes in gold and silver colors and in various strengths. It is easy to find in craft stores and bead stores, often under the brand names Soft Flex, Accuflex, Beadalon, and Acculon. But I do not recommend it for the beginning beader, as it requires tools and crimp beads to seal off. Save it for when you have already made a few sets using a needle and one of the threads described above.

Getting Started: Tools

There are several tools you will need no matter the design of your prayer beads. Some of these you may already have in your tool box, and those will do for a start. Later, those made specifically for jewelry use will give you more precise control.

Chain-nose or flat-nose pliers. This hand tool has flat, tapered ends that come to a point. Use it to pull the tails of beading wire through a crimp bead.

Needle-nose or round-nose pliers. The ends of this set of pliers are rounded and come down to a point. They are sometimes called "rosary pliers" because they are used to make the chain loops that form traditional Catholic rosaries.

Crimping tool. This tool looks like a pair of pliers, but has two holes when it is closed. The first hole has a rounded half and a notched half, and the second hole has two rounded halves. It is used for sealing crimp beads which are used with flexible beading wire.

Wire-cutting tool. A jewelry maker's wire cutter will cut flexible beading wire very close to the beads, but you may be able to make do with one already in your tool box.

You will also need a pair of scissors, a tube of hypo cement or other non-water-soluble glue, and a cloth on which to spread out your beads and other supplies. Most bead stores carry rimmed bead trays with velvet pads that will keep your beads from running off the edge of the table. A rectangle of Velux blanket fabric will do very well, too, and most bead stores carry them for a dollar or two. The long fibers of the Velux grab on to the beads and keep them from rolling around. Alternately, you can cut a rectangle from an old blanket.

For any thread other than large cords or flexible beading wire, a needle is required. Sewing needles will not do. Their eyes are too big to fit through the small holes of most beads. Most beads require a size 10 beading needle, available at most bead, craft, and fabric stores. For beads with tiny holes—like those drilled through most freshwater and dyed pearls—use a smaller needle, like a size 12. These can be a challenge to thread. Invest a dollar or two in a needle threader, also found in most craft, sewing, and bead stores.

*Pearls lie not
on the seashore.
If thou desirest one,
thou must dive for it.*

CHINESE PROVERB

The instructions for making an Anglican and a Catholic rosary are very similar. For the most part, it is only the number and size of beads that is different. Because the Anglican rosary has fewer beads than the Catholic rosary, you may find it easier to start with it first before moving on to the longer Catholic version.

Basic Anglican Rosary

Gather beads in four different sizes. I have included size suggestions below, but they are just that—suggestions. The point is that there should be some *tactile* and *visible* clue to the fingers and eyes about what part of the rosary you are praying on. Forgo using a large bead instead of a cross or charm for your first, basic rosary because it requires a different way of tying it off. Learn the basic way of knotting—the surgeon's knot—first.

You must also decide how many connector beads to use between the different types of beads. Again, I have recommended some numbers, but use as few or as many as you like. I like there to be a larger space between a set of weeks beads and the adjacent cruciform bead than there is between the individual weeks beads. Similarly, I like a larger space between the cross and the invitatory bead and the rest of the rosary.

A rosary means a garden of roses. Think of the rosary as having a stem—the dangling part that ends in a cross or charm—and a path—the circle of beads.

YOU WILL NEED

    1 cross or charm

    1 invitatory bead—size 10–12 mm or larger

    4 cruciform beads—size 8–10 mm

    28 weeks beads—size 6–8 mm

    Connector beads—size 8 or 11 seed beads

    Beading thread

    Size 10 beading needle

    Hypo cement or nonwater-soluble glue

    Small scissors

    Clothespin or small clamp, such as an alligator clip
       or an office binder clip

1. Cut a 4-foot length of thread. Thread needle and bring both ends of thread together for a double strand. Place clothespin or small clamp at the end, leaving about a 4-inch tail.

2. String the cross or charm and move it down to the clothespin or clamp. String the stem of the rosary in the following order: 3–5 connector beads, 1 invitatory bead, 3–5 connector beads, 1 cruciform bead.

3. String the path of the rosary in the following order: 3–5 connector beads, *1 weeks bead, 2–3 connector beads.* Repeat between * and * until there are 7 weeks beads on the thread. *Stop* after the seventh weeks bead is strung. Then string 3–5 connector beads, 1 cruciform bead, and 3–5 connector beads. Repeat between * and * again until another 7 weeks beads have been strung. Then add 3–5 connector beads, 1 cruciform bead, and 3–5 connector beads. Repeat until all weeks and cruciform beads are strung, ending with 3–5 connector beads.

Every time you pray, if your prayer is sincere, there will be new feeling and new meaning in it which will give you fresh courage, and you will understand that prayer is an education.

FYODOR DOSTOEVSKY

4. To close the circle of the rosary, bring the needle back down through the *first* cruciform bead strung and through *all the remaining beads* on the rosary's stem, exiting the bead next to the cross or charm. Pass the needle back through the cross or charm so that both thread tails are exiting the same side of the cross and lying side by side.

5. Remove the clothespin or clamp. Pull threads to draw the beads snug. With both thread tails, make a surgeon's knot around the top of the cross or charm in the following manner.

   a. Hold tails in your right hand and the rosary in the left. Keep the beads snug and bring the tails over the rest of the thread to form a loop that captures the cross or the charm (step 1). Pass the tails through the loop and out once (step 2). Pull the knot tight and snug against the cross (step 3). You may find using a small pointed tool, such as an awl or a small knitting needle, will help move the knot close to the cross or charm.

   b. Repeat step 1, passing the thread through the loop twice (step 4), and pull tight (step 5). The knot should be sandwiched between the cross and the first bead strung.

6. Rethread the tails—one strand at a time if need be—and draw the needle and tails back through the first 5 seeds beads strung and back through the invitatory bead. Clip thread close to the invitatory bead. Thread remaining tail and repeat.

7. Place a small drop of hypo cement on the knot. Let dry.

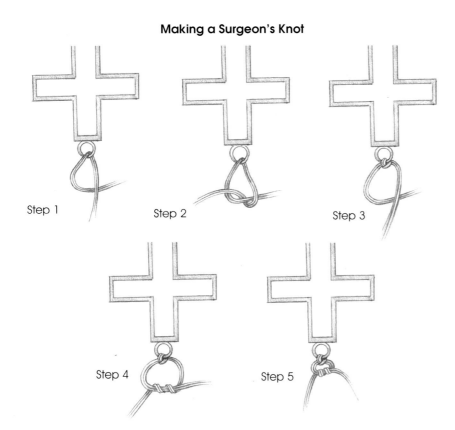

Making a Surgeon's Knot

Step 1

Step 2

Step 3

Step 4

Step 5

Basic Catholic Rosary

This most basic form of the Catholic rosary does not have a medal, but uses a second pass of the thread through the second Our Father bead to draw the circle of the rosary together. So when you use it to pray the traditional Catholic rosary prayers, remember to pray the Fatima Prayer or the Hail Holy Queen Prayer after the third repeat of the last decade on the connector beads.

As with the Basic Anglican Rosary, decide how many connector beads you will use between the types of beads. I have listed some suitable numbers below.

Of all things, guard against neglecting God in the secret place of prayer.

WILLIAM WILBERFORCE

YOU WILL NEED

> 1 crucifix or charm
>
> 53 decade and Hail Mary beads (50 for the decades, 3 for the Hail Marys)—6 mm
>
> 6 Our Father beads—8 mm
>
> Connector beads —size 8 to 11 seed beads
>
> Beading thread
>
> Size 10 beading needle
>
> Hypo cement or nonwater-soluble glue
>
> Small scissors
>
> Clothespin or small clamp, such as an alligator clip or an office binder clip

1. Cut a 5-foot length of thread. Thread needle and bring both ends of thread together to form a double strand. Place clothespin or small clamp at the end, leaving about a 4-inch tail.

2. String the crucifix or charm and move it down to the clothespin or clamp. String the stem of the rosary in the following order: 3–5 connector beads, 1 Our Father bead, 2–3 connector beads, 1 Hail Mary bead, 2–3 connector beads, 1 Hail Mary bead, 2–3 connector beads, 1 Hail Mary bead, 3–5 connector beads, 1 Our Father bead.

3. String the path of the rosary in the following order: 3–5 connector beads, *1 decade bead, 2–3 connector beads.* Repeat between * and * until there are 10 decade beads on the thread. *Stop* after the tenth decade bead is strung. Then string 3–5 connector beads, 1 Our Father bead, and 3–5 connector beads. Repeat between * and * again until another 10 decade beads have been added. Then add 3–5 connector beads, 1 Our Father bead, and 3–5 connector beads. Repeat until all decade and Our Father beads are strung, ending with 3–5 connector beads.

4. To close the circle of the rosary, bring the needle back down through the *second* Our Father bead strung and through *all the remaining beads* on the rosary's stem down to the crucifix or charm. The needle and thread should be exiting the first connector bead strung in step 1. Pass the needle back through the crucifix or charm so that both thread tails are exiting the same side of the crucifix or charm and lying side by side.

5. Remove the clothespin or clamp. Pull threads to draw the beads snug. With both thread tails, make a surgeon's knot as described in step 5 of the Basic Anglican Rosary

6. Rethread the tails—one strand at a time if need be—and draw the needle and tails back through the first 3–5 connector beads strung in step 1, back through the first Our Father bead, and through a few more beads on the stem. Clip thread close to the beads. Thread remaining tail and repeat.

7. Place a small drop of hypo cement on the knot. Let dry.

By adding a few basic wire work techniques, we can add a few simple elements to the basic rosary to make it sturdier.

Intermediate Anglican Rosary

YOU WILL NEED

All of the beads listed for the Basic Anglican Rosary plus:

Flexible beading wire

Flat-nose pliers

Wire-cutting tool

Crimping tool

1 crimp bead large enough to fit 4 strands of your chosen flexible beading wire

Clothespin or small clamp, such as an alligator clip or an office binder clip

*Conceal'd or
unconceal'd
the seed is waiting*

WALT WHITMAN,
SONG OF THE UNIVERSAL

1. Cut a 2-foot length of flexible beading wire. Place clothespin or small clamp at one end, leaving about a 2-inch tail.

2. String the cross or charm and move it down to the clothespin or clamp. String the crimp bead.

   Continue to follow steps 2 through 4 for making a Basic Anglican Rosary as described on page 123. Instead of using thread, you will be using flexible beading wire.

5. Remove the clothespin or small clamp. Using flat-nose pliers, pass *both ends* of flexible beading wire back through the crimp bead and through one or two connector beads on the stem. Pull to snug up all the beads.

6. Use the crimping tool to close the crimp bead:

   a. Place the crimp bead on the first notch of the crimping pliers (the part that is round on one side and notched on the other) and squeeze.

   b. Move the crimp bead to the second notch on the crimping pliers (the part that is rounded on both sides). Rotate the crimp bead 45 degrees so that the creased portion is facing out of the tips of the crimping tool. Squeeze.

7. Use wire cutters to trim the tails of the flexible beading wire close to the beads.

Intermediate Catholic Rosary

Here we will learn to attach a medal between the stem and the path of the rosary.

YOU WILL NEED

All of the beads listed for the Basic Catholic Rosary plus:

A rosary medal with 3 holes

Flexible beading wire

Flat-nose pliers

Wire-cutting tool

Crimping tool

4 crimp beads large enough to fit 2 strands of your chosen flexible beading wire

Clothespin or small clamp, such as an alligator clip or an office binder clip

Make the Stem of the Rosary

1. Cut a 3-foot length of flexible beading wire. String the crucifix or charm and move it down to the end of the wire, leaving a 2-inch tail. String 1 crimp bead. Close the crimp bead as described in step 6 of the Intermediate Anglican Rosary. String 3–5 connector beads, passing them over the tail of the wire and down to the closed crimp bead. Clip the tail close to the connector beads.

2. Continue stringing the beads of the stem, beginning with the first Our Father bead, as described in step 2 of the Basic Catholic Rosary. Finish with 3–5 connector beads and 1 crimp bead.

3. String the bottom hole of the medal on the wire and draw the wire back through the crimp bead, capturing the medal with the wire, and pass the wire back through the 3–5 connector beads. Using flat-nose pliers, pull snug. Use the crimp tool to close the crimp bead. Cut wire close to beads.

Make the Circle of the Rosary

1. String the remaining wire through a top hole of the medal, leaving a 2-inch tail. String 1 crimp bead and pass the tail back through the crimp bead, capturing the medal with the wire. Close the crimp bead. String 3–5 connector beads and pass them over the tail of the wire. Cut wire close to the connector beads. Continue stringing the beads of the rosary circle, beginning with the first decade bead, as described in step 3 of the Basic Catholic Rosary.

2. Close the circle of the rosary by stringing one crimp bead and passing the wire through the remaining hole of medal, capturing the medal with the wire, and pass the wire back through the last 3–5 connector beads strung. Using the flat-nose pliers, pull snug. Close the crimp bead and clip the wire close to the beads.

❧

We can make an Anglican rosary with a medal, too, or use a special jewelry finding called a "Y-connector." Like a rosary medal, a Y-connector is a decorative metal piece that is more or less triangular in shape and has three holes to connect different strands of beads together. Look for Y-connectors in local bead or craft stores and follow the directions for the Intermediate Catholic Rosary, substituting a Y-connector for the rosary medal and using the beads appropriate to the Anglican rosary.

A Chain-Looped Rosary

This is the way the majority of Catholic rosaries found in stores are made, with small wire loops extending from each bead and joined to adjacent beads by linking these loops to each other. This technique eliminates the need for flexible beading wire or other thread, connector beads, and crimp beads. You will need "eye pins," a short length of wire that comes with a loop at one end, like the eye of a needle. This is not a technique for beginners, but it can be mastered with a little practice. You will also need a jump ring—a small metal circle that can be opened and closed—to attach the cross or charm. If you use a Y-connector or medal to connect the rosary path and stem, you will need another three jump rings to attach it to the rest of the rosary.

YOU WILL NEED

All the beads described in the Basic Anglican Rosary or the Basic Catholic Rosary plus:

33 (for the Anglican rosary) or 59 (for the Catholic rosary) eye pins long enough to extend at least 3/8 inch beyond the different sizes of beads

Wire-cutting tool

Needle-nose pliers

Flat-nose pliers

Y-connector or medal (optional)

1–4 jump rings

Praying gives sense, brings wisdom, broadens and strengthens the mind. . . . We can learn more in an hour praying, when praying indeed, than from many hours in the study.

E. M. BOUNDS

Make the Stem of the Rosary

1. Place all stem beads on eye pins. With a wire-cutting tool, cut eye pins to leave a 3/8-inch tail above the beads. Beginning with the invitatory bead (for the Anglican version) or the first Our Father bead (for the Catholic version), bend the tail back against the bead to form a 90-degree angle.

Step 1 Step 2 Step 3 Step 4

2. With the needle-nose pliers, grasp the very tip of the tail of the eye pin at the place along the pliers where the circumference equals that of the other, looped end of the eye pin. Holding the bead with your free hand, rotate the pliers along the tail and toward the bead to form a circle that is the same size of the loop at the other end of the eye pin. *Stop just before the circle is closed.*

3. Slip the looped end of a second eye pin inside the circle you have just formed on the first eye pin. Use the flat-nose pliers to gently squeeze closed the circle of the first eye pin to capture the loop of the second eye pin (step 3). Trim any excess wire. Using both pairs of pliers, position the loop you have just made above the hole of the bead (step 4). Place the cruciform bead or the Hail Mary bead on the second eye pin, and continue steps 1 through 3, arranging the beads of the stem in the order appropriate to the type you are making (Anglican or Catholic).

When all stem beads are connected, pick up a jump ring and grasp it with both the needle-nose pliers and the flat-nose pliers, holding one tool in each hand and placing the small split in the jump ring between the two pliers at the top of the jump ring. Open the jump ring by moving the tool in your *right hand away* from you *at the same time* you move the tool in your *left hand toward* you. Do not pull the jump ring open, as this will weaken it. Place the bottom loop of the medal or Y-connector and the circle of the eye pin extending from the last bead of the stem onto the jump ring. Close the jump ring by reversing the steps you made to open it.

Make the Path of the Rosary

1. Place all path beads on eye pins. With wire-cutting tool, cut the eye pins to leave a 3/8-inch tail above the beads.

2. Open another jump ring. Place a top hole of the medal or Y-connector and the loop of the eye pin for the first weeks bead (for the Anglican version) or the first decade bead (for the Catholic version) on the jump ring. Close the jump ring using the technique described above.

3. Place the first weeks bead (for the Anglican version) or the first decade bead (for the Catholic version) on the eye pin. Follow steps 1–3 for making the stem of the rosary to form a loop and attach the next eye pin and bead. Continue until all the beads of the path of the rosary have been connected. Make and close a loop on the eye pin of the last weeks or decade bead.

4. Open a jump ring. Place the last hole of the medal or Y-connector and the circle of the last bead on the path of the rosary onto the jump ring. Close the jump ring.

*O the blest eyes,
the happy hearts,*

*That see, that know
the guiding
thread so fine,*

*Along the mighty
labyrinth.*

WALT WHITMAN,
SONG OF THE UNIVERSAL

Other Design Options

Now that you have the skills to make basic, intermediate, and advanced rosaries, there are a few further choices available that will open up even more design options.

Decorative Spacers

Try adding additional uncounted spacers made from base or precious metal before and after the larger beads of the rosary. Some possibilities include daisies—small disks of silver or gold—and bead caps—silver or gold cones that bracket a bead.

Toggle Clasp

Instead of a medal or Y-connector, you can use a toggle clasp to join the stem and path of the rosary. The toggle clasp has two parts: a bar and a large circle the bar fits through. Both have a small hole to connect it to the rest of the jewelry. To use it in a rosary, discard the bar and keep the circle. Place a crimp bead after the last bead on the rosary stem. Pass the wire extending from the stem through the circle's small hole and back through the crimp bead and the adjacent connector beads. Close the crimp bead. For the path of the rosary, string 9–11 connector beads (size 11 seed beads work best) and a crimp bead and pass them down the wire leaving a 2-inch tail. Pass the beaded section of wire through the center of the toggle clasp. Pass the tail of the wire back through the crimp bead capturing the toggle clasp in a small loop of beads. Close the crimp bead. String the rest of the path of the rosary,

Prayer and patience and faith are never disappointed.

RICHARD NEWTON

being sure to cover the tail of the wire with connector beads. After all the beads for the path are strung, add another crimp bead and 9–11 connector beads and capture the center of the toggle again, passing the wire back through the crimp bead and under the adjacent connector beads. Pull snug and close the crimp bead.

Large Beads

You may want to use a large bead instead of a cross or charm. Use flexible beading wire only. On the stem of the rosary, begin by stringing one connector bead and one crimp bead. Leave a 2-inch tail. Pass the tail back through the crimp bead only. Close the crimp bead and string the large bead, hiding the rest of the tail inside it. Clip any excess tail close to the bead. The connector bead will catch the large bead and keep it from sliding off the wire. Continue stringing the rest of the rosary.

Knotting between Beads

In this technique knots replace the uncounted connector beads between the counted beads. You can use silk thread that comes in an array of colors on small cards with a needle already attached, or any kind of cording that will pass through your beads.

Cut a length of thread or cord that is two to three times *longer* than the finished rosary will be. This will allow for the thread or cord the knots will take up. Follow the directions for the Basic Anglican Rosary, but tie a loose, over-hand knot (step 1)—the kind you make when you tie your shoes—in place of the connector beads. *Do not tighten the knot.* Use an awl or other tapered tool (some tapestry needles will do) to move the knot along the thread or cord (step 2). Place the knot as close to the counted bead as possible. Pull the knot tight as you remove the awl or needle (step 3). String the next bead and continue until all the beads are strung.

1. Make an overhand knot

2. Insert awl

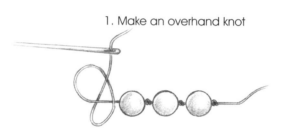

3. Pull thread and pull awl out

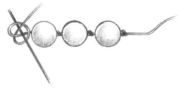

Prayer Bracelets and Prayer Strands

You may want to make shorter versions of the Anglican or Catholic rosary, with only one set of weeks or decades and one or two cruciform beads or Hail Mary beads and a cross, crucifix, or charm. These can be made in the form of bracelets, using elastic thread, or in the form of dangling prayer strands.

Prayer Bracelets

These are shortened versions of a rosary that are elastic and can fit around a wrist. You may want to use smaller beads than you would for a regular rosary, but do not go smaller than a size 8 seed bead for the connector beads, or it will be difficult to get the elastic thread to pass through them. Most bracelets are 7 1/2 inches long, and you should experiment on your wrist to determine how many connector beads to place between the counted beads to reach that length or another length that fits you. A flexible wire needle—a piece of twisted wire with a large, flexible hole that passes through beads—will make threading the beads on the elastic easy. These needles can be found at bead stores, and sometimes are sold with elastic thread. When you pray with the Catholic version, your fingers will have to do some jumping between the beads to get the prayers in, but all of the necessary beads are there.

For an Anglican Prayer Bracelet

> Connector beads—size 8 or larger seed beads
> 1 cross or charm
> 1 invitatory bead
> 2 cruciform beads
> 14 weeks beads
> hypo cement or glue
> clothespin or clamp

1. Cut a 12-inch length of elastic thread. Place clothespin or other clamp on one end, leaving a 3- to 4-inch tail.

2. String beads in the following order: cross or charm, 1–3 seed beads, invitatory bead, 1–3 seed beads, cruciform bead, 1–3 seed beads, *1 weeks bead, 1–3 seed beads.* Repeat between * and * until 7 weeks beads are strung. Add 1–3 seed beads, one cruciform bead, *1–3 seed beads and 1 weeks bead.* Continue between * and * until all beads are strung.

3. Pass the needle back through the first cruciform bead strung and continue through the remaining beads, exiting through the cross. Tie a surgeon's knot, and if possible, pass tail of elastic back through the adjacent beads. Dab knot with glue and let dry. If unable to pass tails of elastic back through adjacent beads, trim tails *after* glue is dry.

For a Catholic Prayer Bracelet

Connector beads—size 8 or larger seed beads

1 crucifix or cross

1 Our Father bead

1 Hail Mary bead (should be different from decade beads)

10 decade beads

1 medal with one hole

hypo cement or glue

clothespin or clamp

1. Cut a 12-inch length of elastic thread. Place clothespin or other clamp on one end, leaving a 3- to 4-inch tail.

2. String beads in the following order: crucifix or cross, 3–5 connector beads, 1 Hail Mary bead, 3–5 connector beads, 1 Our Father bead, 3–5 connector

beads, *1 decade bead, 3–5 connector beads.* Continue between * and * until all beads are strung. Join in a circle and tie a surgeon's knot. If possible, pass the tails of the elastic back through some of the adjacent beads. Dab knot with glue and let dry. If unable to pass tails of elastic back through adjacent beads, trim tails *after* glue is dry.

Prayer Strands

This is the simplest form of prayer beads you can make. The Anglican form consists of just ten beads and a charm, and the Catholic form consists of thirteen beads and a crucifix. Using a lobster claw clasp—the large hinged clasp that joins most necklaces —will allow you to hook it onto a purse strap, a belt loop, or any other place you might want to carry this short, straight line of prayer beads. When you pray, start at the cross, charm, or crucifix as usual, and move up the strand. When you complete your first set of weeks or decades, simply move back down the strand to the cruciform or the Our Father bead and repeat until you are done.

Anglican Prayer Strand

YOU WILL NEED

    1 cross or charm
    1 invitatory bead—size 10–12 mm or larger
    2 cruciform beads—size 8–10 mm
    7 weeks beads—size 6–8 mm

Joseph and Mary walk'd through an orchard good,

where was cherries and berries so red as any blood.

Joseph and Mary walk'd through an orchard green,

where was berries and cherries as thick as might be seen.

THE CHERRY TREE CAROL

Catholic Prayer Strand

YOU WILL NEED

> 1 crucifix or charm
>
> 1 Hail Mary bead
>
> 3 Our Father beads
>
> 10 decades beads
>
> 1 medal with 1 hole

Both Versions

YOU WILL NEED

> Connector beads—size 8 or 11 seed beads
>
> 1 large lobster claw or other clasp
>
> Thread or flexible beading wire
>
> 2 crimp beads, if using wire
>
> Size 10 beading needle, if using thread
>
> hypo cement or glue

1. Cut a length of thread or wire that will allow a 2-inch tail at both ends of the finished strand if using wire, or 4 to 6 inches if using thread.

2. If working with *wire*, string a lobster claw or other clasp and a crimp bead. Pass the tail of the wire back through the crimp bead, capturing the lobster claw or clasp in a small loop and leaving a 2-inch tail. Close the crimp bead. If using *thread*, string the lobster claw or clasp. Tie a surgeon's knot as described in the Basic Anglican Rosary and dab with glue. Let dry.

3. For the Anglican Prayer Strand, string beads in the following order: 1 cruciform, *3 connector beads, 1 weeks bead,* repeating between * and * until all 7 weeks beads are strung. Add 3 connector beads, 1 cruciform bead,

Words form the thread on which we string our experiences.

ALDOUS HUXLEY

and the invitatory bead. For a Catholic Prayer Strand, string beads in the following order: 1 Our Father bead, *3 connector beads, 1 decades bead,* repeating between * and * until all decades beads are strung. Add 3 connector beads, 1 Our Father bead, 1 medal, 3 connector beads, 1 Hail Mary bead, 3 connector beads, and 1 Our Father bead. If using *wire*, add crimp bead and cross, charm, or crucifix. Insert tail of wire into crimp bead, capturing the cross, charm, or crucifix in a small loop. Pull the wire snug and close the crimp bead. Pass the tail under 3 or more beads on the strand. Cut wire close to beads. If using *thread*, add cross, charm, or tie a surgeon's knot as described in the Basic Anglican Rosary. Rethread the tails—one strand at a time if need be—and draw the thread back through the last connector beads strung. Clip thread close to the beads. Thread remaining tail and repeat. Place a small drop of hypo cement on the knot. Let dry.

Other Forms of Prayer Beads

A Lutheran Rosary

The Evangelical Lutheran Church of America has suggested the use of a Lutheran rosary as a tool to reflection and contemplation during the Lenten season. It has a cross and forty-seven beads—three smaller beads and one larger bead on the stem, forty-two on the path consisting of one smaller bead for each weekday of Lent plus six larger beads for each Sunday. You can make your own version of this rosary by following any of the techniques for the Anglican rosary and changing the numbers and types of beads accordingly. The church has suggested prayers and intentions for the different days of Lent, which can be found on its website at www.elca.org/communication/rosary.html. A free booklet describing how to use this rosary is available from www.lutheranprayerbeads.com.

When you examine the lives of the most influential people who have ever walked among us, you discover one thread that winds through them all. They have been aligned first with their spiritual nature and only then with their physical selves.

ALBERT EINSTEIN

Pearls of Life

This set of ecumenical prayer beads, developed by the Swedish Lutheran bishop Martin Lonnebo, consists of eighteen different beads, or "pearls," each a symbol of our relationship with God. The meaning of the beads is described in chapter three. The Pearls of Life is a simple circlet of beads and can be made by simply stringing the beads in the appropriate order and tying a knot. The sizes of beads below are merely a suggestion.

YOU WILL NEED

1 God bead—round gold bead, approx. 12–15mm

6 Pearls of Silence—oblong wood beads, approx. 12 mm

1 I Pearl—round white bead, approx. 6–8mm

1 Baptism Pearl—round white bead, approx. 10mm

1 Desert Pearl—round beige bead, approx. 8–10mm

1 Serenity Pearl—round blue bead, approx 8–10mm

2 Love Pearls—round red beads, approx. 6–8mm

3 Mystery Beads—round white beads, approx. 6mm

1 Night Pearl—round black bead, approx. 8–10mm

1 Resurrection Pearl—round white bead, approx. 10mm

1. String the beads on elastic cord or thread in the following order: 1 God bead, 1 Pearl of Silence, 1 Baptism Pearl, 1 Pearl of Silence, 1 Night Pearl, 3 Mystery Beads, 2 Love Beads, 1 Pearl of Silence, the Serenity Pearl, 1 Pearl of Silence, 1 Desert Pearl, 1 Pearl of Silence, the Resurrection Pearl, the I-Pearl, and 1 Pearl of Silence. Tie the cord or thread together with a surgeon's knot and place a drop of glue on the knot. Let dry and trim the tails close to the beads.

The Pearls of Life are a free-form set of prayer beads, so they can be used in any fashion and with any prayers the user chooses. Martin Lönnebo has written a book about the Pearls of Life describing their use. It can be purchased from his website at www.wreathoflife.com.

Perhaps none of these established forms of prayer beads is right for your prayer life. Feel free to experiment with the beading techniques described here to create your own unique sets of prayer beads on which you pray any prayers in any way you like. Select beads that say something about your own spiritual quest. The choice is yours and the possibilities, like faith, are endless.

Rosary crosses and charms.

CHAPTER TEN

GIVING THE GIFT OF PRAYER BEADS

All night she spent in bidding of her bedes
And all the day in doing good and godly deeds.

—EDMUND SPENSER, *THE FAERIE QUEEN*

*P*rayer beads are personal and intimate. Their use is an expression of the upward and outward yearning of the heart and soul toward the divine. But not everyone who prays will want to or need to pray in this way. Many people already have their own deep and satisfying prayer practices.

So giving someone a set of prayer beads *unasked* could be taken as rather presumptuous. The intended recipient might think you don't think he or she is devout enough, or has a relationship with God that isn't what it should be. Those are judgments no one can or should make—and judgments no one should be on the receiving end of. Faith of any kind is a very personal and private part of life for many people. Spontaneously giving someone a set of unasked-for prayer beads could cross some kind of line in your relationship

If attentiveness and prayer are daily joined together, they become like a fire-bearing chariot, raising us to heaven.

PHILOTHEUS OF SINAI

with that person making the would-be recipient feel uncomfortable, criticized, or somehow lacking in faith.

Of course, there are plenty of people who would love to have prayer beads and would use them unreservedly. You can almost ensure this kind of response if you answer a few questions about the person you think might like a set of their own. What do you know about this person's faith life? Has he or she ever expressed a desire to go deeper in his or her faith practices? Does the person come from a faith background that has a tradition of prayer beads? Do you know if he or she has a personal prayer practice *outside* of church? Do you have any reason to think he or she may want to begin such a practice?

And there are some difficult questions you should ask yourself, too. Foremost among them is what is your real motivation behind wanting to give this person a set of prayer beads? Do you really believe it is a gift that would truly benefit the recipient, or are you more interested in showcasing your new beading skills and prayer practice? Are you motivated by a truly generous, loving spirit, or are you seeking attention and approval?

These are not easy questions because the answers can sometimes force us to look at an unpleasant reality about ourselves. I suggest you pray on them—on your own prayer beads, of course—before you decide whether or not to make and give away a set to someone else. When I have a question about what action I should take, I find Saint Thomas Aquinas's prayer "For Ordering a Life Wisely," included here in chapter six (page 82), is particularly good for helping me discern my path.

After you have asked these questions of yourself, there is one other thing to do, if possible, before making and giving away a set of beads. I have found one of the best ways to find out if a gift of prayer beads would be appropriate for someone is to just whip out my Anglican rosary and show them to the person. This is not something I just do randomly, but only if the person has some-how indicated to me that he or she is a person of faith. Perhaps they've mentioned the congregation they belong to, a spiritual book they have read, or the fact that they pray. When the time is right—over lunch, on a drive, during a walk—I'll dig through my purse for something and casually pull out my prayer beads and lay them where they can see them. "What's this?" they inevitably ask, lured by the color and shine of the beads. Then I tell them it is my Anglican rosary and briefly explain how I use it. Some people will just say, "Neat," or "Oh," and put them down and move on to another subject. No prayer beads for them. Others will say, "Wow," and start asking a lot of questions. When they get around to, "Where did you get them," I begin thinking of the set I will make for them.

When you do decide a gift of prayer beads is right, try to find out what colors, beads, and charm will be most suitable for the recipient. Do they find solace in a garden or in nature? Maybe a vine-covered cross or a leaf charm would be best on the stern of the rosary. What color is their bedroom? This is usually the part of the house where we find the most sanctuary and solace, so the colors there tend to be what the person finds most soothing and pleasant. Then choose your beads accordingly. Look for clues. Maybe they always wear red—like my friend Daniela, for whom I made a set of bright red prayer beads. Or perhaps they go for more tropical colors, like my friend Sandy, a long-time church-goer for whom I made a set of pink and turquoise prayer beads with a silver cross at its end. Use your eyes and your common sense. Ask their friends and family about their favorite things, if you can.

Once you have made a set of prayer beads as a gift, you will need to include instructions on how to use them and a prayer or two. You can make this up on your own, or you can include the instructions in this chapter. They

Prayer and helplessness are inseparable. Only those who are truly helpless can pray.

OLE HALLESBY,
WATCH AND PRAY

are for an Anglican rosary, but a little creative adaptation in the number of repetitions of the prayers can make them suitable for other prayer beads, too. You'll also want to copy the diagram of the Anglican rosary on page 34. Instructions for a Catholic rosary are available in many religious bookstores and come printed on small cards, perfect for carrying in a pocket or purse. They can also be found on the Internet, on sites such as Catholic Online (www.catholic.org/clife/prayers/rosary.php) and Catholic Information Service (www.kofc.org/un/eb/en/publications/cis/devotional/rosary.html). Feel free to copy the next few pages onto some nice cardstock and attach them with a coordinating ribbon to the beads, or slip them into the envelope of a gift or greeting card you will include.

The Anglican Rosary

History of the Anglican Rosary

Almost every world religion has some method of counting prayers. The Anglican Rosary was developed in the 1980s as an aid for Protestants seeking a contemplative prayer tool. It is a hybrid of the Catholic rosary and the Orthodox Christian prayer rope.

The Symbolism of the Anglican Rosary

The Anglican rosary has thirty-three beads, one for each year of Christ's life, and a cross. The number seven, represented by the weeks, is associated with perfection and the divine. The circle formed by the four sets of weeks beads and the four cruciform beads can represent a range of things: the four Gospels, the four seasons of the year, the four elements of nature (earth, fire, wind, and water).

Helplessness is the real secret and the impelling power of prayer.

OLE HALLESBY

Praying the Anglican Rosary

The beauty of the Anglican rosary is that there are no set prayers for it, no right or wrong way to pray it. You can say any prayers you like on each of the beads. To start, grasp the cross or charm and say the prayer assigned to it. Then move to the invitatory bead and say its assigned prayer. Next, move into the circle of the rosary with the first cruciform bead, reciting its prayer, and move on to the weeks beads and the other cruciform beads, saying those prayers. You may move through the cruciforms and weeks as many times as you like, though three times is recommended. Finish the rosary by moving back to the invitatory bead, repeating its prayer and then do the same on the cross or charm.

As you pray, try to breathe and relax, focusing only on the prayer. Let it lull you and fill you. This will take practice. Keep at it.

Some Prayers for the Anglican Rosary

Below are some prayers suitable for the different beads of the Anglican rosary. Mix and match as you see fit. Then go in search of your own in the Bible, in the Book of Common Prayer, or in any collection of prayers. Feel free to compose your own as well.

On the Cross or Charm

> The Lord's Prayer
> In the Name of God, Father, Son, and Holy Spirit. Amen.

On the Invitatory Bead

> O God make speed to save me,
> O Lord make haste to help me.

Prayer is the expression of a wish to God and, since God searches the heart, the conceiving even of the wish is prayer in God's eyes.

GERARD MANLEY HOPKINS

Glory to the Father, and to the Son, and to the Holy Spirit: As it was in the
  beginning, is now, and will be forever. Amen.

O God, early in the morning I cry to you.
Help me to pray and to concentrate my thoughts on you:
I cannot do this alone.
—Prayer of Dietrich Bonhoeffer

God grant me the serenity
to accept the things I cannot change;
courage to change the things I can;
and wisdom to know the difference.
—The Serenity Prayer

Let the words of my mouth and the meditation of my heart be acceptable
  in your sight, O Lord, my rock and my redeemer.
—Psalm 19:14

On The Cruciform Beads

Holy God,
Holy and Mighty,
Holy Immortal One,
Have mercy upon me.

*No cord or cable
can draw so forcibly,
or bind so fast,
as love can do with
a single thread.*

ROBERT BURTON

On The Weeks Beads

Lord Jesus Christ, Son of God,
Have mercy on me, a sinner.
—The Jesus Prayer

And all shall be well, and all shall be well, and all manner of thing
    shall be well.
—Prayer of Julian of Norwich

I lift up my eyes to the hills;
From where will my help come?
My help comes from the Lord,
who made heaven and earth.
—Psalm 121:1–2

(*Recite one per bead*)
Grant unto me, my God, that I may direct my heart to you.
Give to me a watchful heart.
Give to me a noble heart.
Give to me a resolute heart.
Give to me a stalwart heart.
Give to me a temperate heart.
Give to me a loving heart.
—adapted from St. Thomas Aquinas

Rosary beads and crosses.

CHAPTER ELEVEN

RESOURCES FOR BEADING AND PRAYING

But all may be done through prayer—almighty prayer,
I am ready to say—and why not? For that it is almighty
is only through the gracious ordination of the God
of love and truth. O then, pray, pray, pray!

—WILLIAM WILBERFORCE, A LETTER TO HIS SON, 1823

There are more bead and prayer resources out there than I can reasonably fit in this book.

To find just the right beads for you, poke around. Buy a beading magazine and look through the advertisements. Open your local Yellow Pages and look up "beads." To gather more prayers, go to the library and sift through the many wonderful prayer books and anthologies available. Ask your pastor where he or she looks when in need of a good prayer. The resources listed below are just some of my favorites and should be a good starting point.

Prayer Books and Prayer Anthologies

I have listed all the prayer books and prayer anthologies I consulted during the writing of this book in the bibliography. But if I had to take three of these to a desert island, one of them would surely be *Women's Uncommon Prayers: Our Lives Revealed, Nurtured, Celebrated* for its prayers for quite literally every need—birth, miscarriage, death, marriage, self-image, abuse—you name it, all of them written by women in the church, both lay and clergy. Another to go along would be *The Doubleday Prayer Collection: Over 1,300 Prayers for All Occasions*, edited by Mary Batchelor, which is especially fine for the general categories of prayer like worship, thanksgiving, praise, and so much more. And for a rich source for old prayers from many Christian paths I would choose *2,000 Years of Prayer*, compiled by Michael Counsell.

But I could not go to my island without the luscious tapestry of prayer found in Phyllis Tickle's *The Divine Hours* series, a guide to the Daily Office of the church for individual prayer. These books include *Prayers for Spring, Prayers for Autumn and Wintertime* and *Prayers for Summertime*. The prayers she has lovingly collected and, in some cases, composed, connect us, through their quotidian use by people around the world, to a vast community of the faithful. Many are appropriate for prayer bead use.

Prayer Bead Retailers

Perhaps you'd like to buy a ready-made set and get started. Here are some places to buy sets of prayer beads. Some are ministries and nonprofits, others sell their beads for profit. I have specified where I can.

You know the value of prayer: it is precious beyond all price. Never, never neglect it.

Sir Thomas Buxton

A Rosary for All Christians

www.arosaryforall.com

Founder Joney Ferguson comes from a jewelry-making family and has been making Anglican rosaries since 1995. Some of her designs have been carried by the museum store at the Washington National Cathedral. She is also available for free Anglican rosary workshops within driving distance of her home in Dallas. She can be reached at 214-349-0065 or by e-mail at Joney@arosaryforall.com.

GiGi Beads

www.gigibeads.net/prayerbeads/saints

This is the online store of Gabriele Whittier, a member of Trinity Episcopal Church in Bethlehem, Pennsylvania, where there is a thriving prayer bead ministry. Gabriele learned about the Anglican rosary from a friend and soon decided she had to make some. She has dozens of Anglican, ecumenical, and Catholic rosaries for sale, as well as chaplets and prayer bracelets. Many are made with specific constituencies in mind, including soldiers, animal lovers, and children. She also does custom orders. Check out her links page for some great rosary prayers. Contact her at gaby@gigibeads.net.

Praxis: Resources for Spiritual Formation and Contemplative Living

www.praxisofprayer.com

Founded by the Rev. Lynn Bauman, the creator of the Anglican rosary, Praxis is a small contemplative ecumenical community of Christians located in Telephone, Texas. They make and sell "the original handmade Anglican rosary" using semiprecious stones and a San Damiano cross ($25) as well as Catholic rosaries ($50) and Orthodox prayer ropes ($75). They also offer Bauman's book, *The Anglican Rosary*. Contact them at 903-664-4310, praxis@netexas.net.

The Rosary Shop

www.rosaryshop.com

This online retailer, based in McMinnville, Maryland, is Catholic-oriented and features Catholic rosary kits that could also be converted to the Anglican format by leaving off some beads. Contact them at 1-800-738-0538.

Solitaries of DeKoven

www.solitariesofdekoven.org

This Episcopal community is organized around a core group of hermits who live secluded on a retreat outside the Texas panhandle town of Santa Anna. They spend their days in contemplation, performing the Daily Offices of the church, intercessory prayer for the world and the church, and in manual labor. As a way to support this lifestyle, they make beautiful Anglican rosaries and offer them for sale on their website. Contact them via e-mail at info@solitariesofdekoven.org.

Local Bead Shops

My first choice for buying beads is my local bead shop. They usually offer a wide variety of beads that reflect the taste and whimsy of the owner, a knowledgeable staff, and an array of classes and other resources to help you out. Here are a few ways to help you find a bead shop near you.

BeadShopFinder.com

www.beadshopfinder.com

   This website is sponsored by three very fine jewelry-making magazines—*Bead & Button, BeadStyle,* and *Art Jewelry* and allows you to search for independently owned bead stores within a one hundred mile radius of the city of your choice. The site has hundreds of stores in its database and lists shop locations, contact information, and website, if applicable, and sometimes a map and directions to the store.

Beadwork's Stop to Shop Directory

www.interweave.com/bead/beadwork_magazine/stop_to_shop.asp

   Interweave Press's *Beadwork* magazine maintains a shop directory of independently owned bead shops in most states and Canada. Listings include street addresses, contact information, and Internet addresses, if applicable, and direct links to websites. This last feature is especially nice because it allows you to see a store's merchandise before investing your time in a shopping trip.

Soft Flex Company

www.softflexcompany.com

   This company, based in Sonoma, California, makes excellent beading wire. On its website it has a shop locator that allows you to search within a 250-mile radius of any zip code. The locator provides store name, location, contact information, website address, if applicable, and usually a map. Stores listed are both independently owned bead shops and chain stores. Their common factor is that they sell Soft Flex.

He who does not pray when the sun shines knows not how to pray when the clouds arise.

William Edward
Biederwolf

Online Bead and Jewelry-Making Retailers

You can also surf the web for everything you need to make prayer beads—but you can't touch the beads to see how they will feel before buying them. Again, there are more online retailers of beads than I can possibly mention. Here are a few that are known for their selection and service.

Fire Mountain Gems & Beads

www.firemountaingems.com

Fire Mountain, based in Grants Pass, Oregon, has everything for beading, from basic glass seed beads to gemstone and semiprecious beads including turquoise, garnet, and jasper and everything in between. They are very highly regarded in the beading community and are known for their selection, speed, and customer service. The company sells both online and via its free 400-plus page catalog that features dozens of beading ideas, including many stringing projects that could serve as inspiration for prayer beads. Also helpful is that almost all the catalog items are pictured at actual size, making it easier to see how several different kinds of beads will look together. They also have a very good selection of crosses in pewter, sterling silver, and vermeil, a kind of gold plate. Especially nice for prayer beads are the affirmation charms—22 mm. sterling silver circles with words such as "faith," "hope," "grace," and "love" engraved on them. To request a catalog, call 1-800-355-2137.

The only way to pray is to pray; and the only way to pray well is to pray much. If one has no time for this, then one must at least pray regularly. But the less one prays, the worse it goes.

JOHN CHAPMAN

FusionBeads.com

www.fusionbeads.com

This Seattle, Washington–based online retailer sells Swarovski crystals and pearls, Czech and Venetian lampwork beads, fire-polished glass beads, precious metal beads, and natural material beads. They also offer findings, charms, pendants, and jewelry-making wire and tools. Particularly nice is their selection of pendants, made from shells, resin, ceramic, glass, and metal in a rainbow of colors and many different sizes and shapes. Quite a few could take the place of a more traditional cross on a set of prayer beads, but be sure and check the dimensions of the pendant before ordering. The website has especially good directions with full color photographs for some of the jewelry-making techniques discussed in this book, including crimping, knotting, wire wrapping, and attaching a charm. Look at the website under "Beading Techniques." Customer service can be reached at 1-888-781-3559.

Rings & Things

www.rings-things.com

This bead retailer is based in Spokane, Washington, and has been in business since the early 1970s. They are a traveling bead shop, staging "BeadTour" shows in cities across the country. Their website lists all scheduled locations and dates. They have a wide, though not comprehensive, selection of beads, with a good array of African trade beads, beads from India, and colored glass assortments. Their selection of bone pendants is also very good. Be sure and explore the "Jewelry Info" section on their website, which is full of interesting facts and history about beads, gemstones, and jewelry making. Contact 1-800-366-2156.

National Craft Retailers

Not everyone is lucky enough to have a great bead store nearby. In that case, check out your local craft and hobby store. In general, their bead and jewelry-making selection is not as broad or comprehensive as that of an independently owned bead shop, but there are still some good finds. Here are some national chains that also allow you to browse, if not shop, via the Internet.

Jo-Ann Fabric and Crafts

www.joann.com/

This online outlet of the national chainstore known primarily for its fabrics has a jewelry and beading section that has everything from tools to beading wire and features beads of glass, plastic, wood, and other materials. The website allows you to find a Jo-Ann store near you or to shop online.

Michael's

www.michaels.com

With more than nine hundred stores in the U.S. and Canada, this company claims to be North America's largest arts and crafts retailer. Stores generally have two or more aisles dedicated to jewelry making, offering beads, tools, wire, findings, and how-to books. One very nice feature of this store is its Bead Gallery line of beads—more than two hundred varieties of glass, wood, shell, freshwater pearls, and beads from seeds, 5 to 18 mm in size and in a range of colors. They are sold in strands of about twenty to twenty-five beads retailing for $3.99 or $5.99 each, which makes them ideal for an inexpensive set of prayer beads. Bead Gallery beads are usually found on a kiosk in the store. Michaels does not sell to customers online, but its website shows all jewelry-making supplies, including beads, carried by its bricks-and-mortar stores and has a store search option to locate a store by city, state, and zip code.

Online Instruction Sites

The primary purpose of this book has been to introduce people to the use of different kinds of rosaries and other prayer beads. I am first and foremost a writer, not a beading teacher. So if my directions have not been complete enough or clear enough for every reader, there are several websites that have detailed beading and jewelry-making instructions, most with photographs and diagrams, that may be of use.

About.com

www.about.com

This information clearinghouse has all kinds of instructional articles on jewelry making, including a fine section on bead stringing written by Tammy Powley. Go to the main web address and enter "Getting Started: Bead Stringing" in the search window. If that doesn't work, enter this address: http://jewelrymaking.about.com/od/gettingstarted/a/122404.htm.

Artbeads.com

www.artbeads.com

This online retailer has a detailed "Learning Center" that both shows and explains many jewelry-making techniques. Particularly good are the instructions for knotting between pearls (or beads) and how to thread a small-eyed needle. The directions for making a basic wire loop are very good, and the accompanying pictures will be especially helpful for those who need a visual aid.

If you wish to experience peace, provide peace for another.

Tenzin Gyatso, the 14th Dalai Lama

Fire Mountain Gems & Beads

www.firemountaingems.com

The "Resources" category on this online retailer's website has a range of informational pages, but the best are a designer's gallery full of inspiring ideas, an "EncycloBEADia" that contains bead charts, FAQs, and articles about beads and jewelry making. A "Beading How-To's" section is full of tips from customers, like how to stow a project in process (stick the needle in a foam curler and snap it shut on the thread!) and how to easily thread a needle (cut the thread on an angle).

The Soft Flex Company

www.softflexcompany.com

This manufacturer of beading wire and cords has an excellent section on its website showing how to make an "8 knot," otherwise known as a surgeon's knot, which is recommended for use with Soft-Flex wire. It also has everything you ever wanted to know about crimping, including a fabulous chart that shows what size crimp bead works best with each size of beading wire. Go to the website and move your cursor over "School of Design" and click on "Tips & Tricks."

And it is this the Father wills: He seeks daily intercourse with His children in listening to and granting their petitions.

Andrew Murray

AFTERWORD

Tears are the prayer-beads of all of us, men and women,
because they arise from a fullness of the heart.

—Edward Hays, *Pray All Ways*

$\mathcal{I}$ am no paragon of prayer. That is not to say that God and I haven't had a long relationship. I have known God since I was a small girl in Sunday school. But it has been an on-again, off-again tortured affair—I might even say it is a love-hate relationship. Just when I get to a point where my faith seems to blossom, something happens, either in world events or in my own personal life, that makes me recoil from God in anger and shock. September 11, 2001. Five miscarried pregnancies. The aftermath of Hurricane Katrina. But I have always, somehow, eventually found my way back. God and I seem to be connected by a bungee cord—in times of pain and frustration I jump away from him, stretching the limit of our bond to the utmost, before I am somehow, ultimately, pulled back.

What happened during the writing of this book is a perfect illustration of that relationship. When I was first asked to write this book, I couldn't say yes fast enough. I had already written *Fabric of Faith: A Guide to the Prayer Quilt Min-*

istry, about how to make and use prayer quilts. But I am not an avid quilter, so as much as I loved meeting and working with the gifted and generous people who made these quilts with prayer in every stitch, I felt more of an observer of than a participant in their craft. But I felt it would be different with prayer beads. I have been a beader for more than ten years, so I know beads in a way I didn't know quilts. I have spent more money and time than I want my family to know on stringing, weaving, wire wrapping, and otherwise manipulating the little suckers.

Before I had the book contract signed, I made my first Anglican rosary. It had turquoise blue faceted glass beads, four leaf-green Venetian glass beads, and because I didn't have a cross lying around and was too eager to make a trip to the bead store, a large round, flat blue Venetian glass bead for a cross. A quick search on the Internet turned up a few prayers and I was on my way.

And what a way it was. From my first sitting with the beads, I was hooked. The weight of the beads and their cool surfaces felt like a balm in my hands. I quickly found the regular rhythm and the repetition of the prayers carried me off to a place of quiet contemplation I had not visited before. They seemed to seep into me, staying with me as a kind of pleasant lull after my prayer session was over. For months, during the first stages of writing this book, I used my Anglican rosary once and sometimes twice a day. I compiled prayers for it from the Psalms and hymns, committing many to memory. I took my new rosary everywhere I went—on walks and hikes, on business trips, on retreats, on vacations. I used them everywhere—on public transportation, in church pews, at the communion rail, in my car, in airplanes and airports, in bed before getting up in the morning and going to sleep at night.

During this time, I had a growing and thrilling feeling that I was finally breaking down the walls I had erected between God and me. Praying daily this way gave me a sense of his presence I had not felt before, a kind of gut feeling that he was, after all, really *with me*. Why, I thought, hadn't I tried daily counted prayer before, beads or no beads? I began to see the assignment to write this book as some grand plan of God's to move in my life.

Then, the bungee cord gave a yank. Halfway through the writing of this book, someone I was close to, a mentor and a friend, became very ill. More than anyone I have met, Sandy Olson was a person I would describe as a true Christian. She lived what Jesus taught, always putting others before herself, always seeking and finding God's hand in her life and in the world. She prayed, I am sure, daily. Sandy had been ill for many years, spending weeks at a time in the hospital for one or more of her handful of chronic ailments. But I never heard her utter one word of self pity. When her illnesses confined her to home or bed or hospital, her first thought was always how she might be letting other people down because she was temporarily grounded.

When I told Sandy about the subject of this book, her elfin face lit up behind her glasses. Of course, she said, prayer beads. Why *can't* we all use prayer beads? She kept up with my progress as I wrote, and was my biggest cheerleader throughout. Last spring, as my deadline began to loom on the not-so-distant horizon, Sandy's always fragile health took a serious hit. She was in and out of the hospital, on and off some heavy-duty drugs, up and down as her health permitted. The last time she entered the hospital, her friends knew things were bad. We felt powerless. I could not do much for her besides pray. And I could make her an Anglican rosary for her to use, too. Like mine, hers was turquoise—her favorite color—with salmon pink separator beads, another of her favorite tropical shades. I took them to her in the hospital, placing them in her hands as she lay in bed trying not to moan or complain. She said she loved them, but I could tell she was in too much pain to really focus on them. I put them in her bedside drawer, then took out mine. As we chatted through her bouts of pain, I fingered them silently, reciting the Jesus Prayer: Lord, Jesus Christ, have mercy on her. Lord, Jesus Christ, have mercy on her.

For weeks, I prayed my Anglican rosary every day for Sandy. But she did not improve, and finally, she was out of options. She slipped into unconsciousness—among her last words were a concern that she was putting her friends to too much trouble—and a number of us gathered in her room before the doctors disconnected her ventilator. In the hour it took her to leave us, we alternately prayed, sang hymns, and told funny "Sandy stories" as we stood in a circle around her bed. In my hands, I was clutching my Anglican rosary, praying the Jesus Prayer for her, over and over.

When she was gone, we friends started gathering her things. In her bedside table, I found the box with her Anglican rosary inside. I turned to her pastor, a beautiful soul who had really helped Sandy make a graceful journey to God, and asked if he would like to have them. He suggested that she be cremated with them, and placed them in her hands just before they wheeled her body away. I just stood there and cried.

When I left the hospital and got into my car, I looked at the Anglican rosary I still held in my hand. So much for this nonsense, I thought. God does not hear us, God does not love us, and God is certainly not *with us* if he could let someone as beautiful as Sandy die. I put the beads away in a pocket of my purse, giving the zipper a harder pull than was absolutely necessary.

Many will read this and think that I have a very immature faith, to hope that God will do what I want, to be unable to see that God's work was in the sparing of Sandy many more months or years of an illness from which she would not recover. I do not disagree. I am simply stating what I felt, not what I knew. At that moment, I was flying as far away from God as I could possibly get at the end of my bungee cord.

I stayed at that remove for months. I did not pick up my Anglican rosary, I did not make any more Anglican rosaries, I did not sit down to work on this book. I simply sat and stewed, furious with God for taking Sandy. But my deadline didn't go away. Eventually, I would have to pick up my Anglican rosary again to get the book done.

Then one morning, I was drying my hair at the bathroom mirror and planning my day. I should work on the book, I thought. But I don't want to. I don't want to because I am too angry at God to write about the value of praying to him. And then it hit me. Sandy, of all people, would want me to tell people just that. Sandy, a woman with a real reason to be angry with God, never was. She would not want me to be angry for her sake. Sandy, who never gave in to the notion that prayer was futile, despite decades of illness, would want me to finish this book. She would want me to pick up my Anglican rosary. She would want me to pray again.

I put the hairdryer down, my hair half finished and unbrushed, found my purse and opened the zipper pocket that had remained closed all this time. The prayer beads felt familiar to my fingers. What to pray? By this point, with lack of practice, the prayers I had memorized had flown from my head. Except for one. "Lord, Jesus Christ, have mercy on me."

Today, I pray again, every day. One or more of my many rosaries is always somewhere near me, in a purse, in a pocket, in a drawer. And the bungee cord between God and me is springing back. It isn't as short as I'd like, but with prayer and practice and with a good grip on my prayer beads, it is getting there, step by step.

I am writing this so that you will know that you do not have to be a perfect person of faith to pray with prayer beads. You just have to try to *have* faith, to be open to the possibility that God really is with us, despite the travails that will inevitably be a part of our lives and the lives of those we love. I am trying to be open to that. And I am trying to live my life in the example of my friend Sandy—with caring for others, trust in the goodness of the world, and, above all, faith in the loving nature of God, who will always be linked to all of us, like so many beads on a string.

This was proved to me about six months after Sandy died. She left me her antique bed, a big, gorgeous wooden box of a thing, and my husband and I went to her house to collect it. As we were taking it apart, I heard something small and metallic fall on the uncarpeted floor. Thinking it was one of the screws that held the bed together, I bent down to retrieve it. Instead, I found a small heart-shaped charm that had apparently fallen between the bed slats. On one side, it showed a pair of praying hands and a small cross. On the back it was engraved with something I think Sandy wanted me to know: "God answers prayer."

AN INVITATION

I have so enjoyed the process of exploration and experimentation with prayer beads that the writing of this book has set me on that I plan to continue it online. I invite you to join me on my prayer bead journey—and to share with me some experiences of your own—at the *Bead One, Pray Too* blog, www.kimberlywinston.wordpress.com. There I will be writing about prayer beads and will offer more information about their different forms and prayers. I also hope to expand on the instructions for making them started here and to share pictures of the many prayer beads that you and I make. Please join me in this conversation.

BIBLIOGRAPHY

Appleton, George, ed. *The Oxford Book of Prayer*. New York: Oxford University Press, 1985.

The Aquinas Prayer Book: The Prayers and Hymns of St. Thomas Aquinas. Manchester, NH: Sophia Institute Press, 1993.

Arico, Carl. *A Taste of Silence: A Guide to the Fundamentals of Centering Prayer*. New York: Continuum Publishing, 1999.

Batchelor, Mary, ed. *The Doubleday Prayer Collection: Over 1,300 Prayers for All Occasions*. New York: Bantam Doubleday Dell, 1992.

Bauman, Lynn C. *The Anglican Rosary*. Telephone, TX: Praxis, 2001.

The Book of Common Prayer. New York: Oxford University Press, 1990.

Cahill, Thomas. *The Desire of the Everlasting Hills: The World Before and After Jesus*. New York: Nan A. Talese/Anchor Books, 1999.

———. *The Gifts of the Jews*. New York: Nan A. Talese/Anchor Books, 1998.

———. *How the Irish Saved Civilization*. New York: Nan A. Talese/Anchor Books, 1995.

Campbell, Jean. *Getting Started String Beads*. Loveland, CO: Interweave Press, 2005.

Coles, Janet, and Robert Budwig. *Beads: An Exploration of Bead Traditions Around the World.* New York: Simon & Schuster, 1997.

Counsell, Michael, ed. *2,000 Years of Prayer.* Harrisburg, PA.: Morehouse Publishing, 1999.

Cunningham, Scott. *Cunningham's Encyclopedia of Crystal, Gem & Metal Magic.* Woodbury, MN: Llewellyn Publications, 2006.

Davies, Horton, ed. *Communion of the Saints: Prayers of the Famous.* Grand Rapids, MI: Eerdmans Publishing, 1990.

De Waal, Esther. *The Celtic Way of Prayer: The Recovery of the Religious Imagination.* New York: Doubleday, 1997.

French, R. M., trans. *The Way of a Pilgrim and a Pilgrim Continues His Way.* San Francisco, CA: Harper San Francisco, 1998.

Furlong, Monica, ed. *Women Pray: Voices Through the Ages, from Many Faiths, Cultures and Traditions.* Woodstock, VT: SkyLight Paths, 2001.

Geitz, Elizabeth Rankin et al, eds. *Women's Uncommon Prayers: Our Lives Revealed, Nurtured, Celebrated.* Harrisburg, PA: Morehouse Publishing, 2000.

The Glenstal Book of Prayer: A Benedictine Prayer Book. Dublin, Ireland: Columbia Press, 2001.

Goodwin, Rufus. *Give Us This Day: The Story of Prayer.* Hudson, NY: Lindesfarne Books, 1999.

Harvey, Andrew, ed. *The Essential Mystics: Selections from the World's Great Wisdom Traditions.* San Francisco, CA: Harper San Francisco, 1996.

Jensen, Jane Richardson, and Patricia Harris-Watkins. *She Who Prays: A Woman's Interfaith Prayer Book.* Harrisburg, PA: Morehouse Publishing, 2005.

Kenner, Corrine. *Crystals for Beginners.* Woodbury, MN: Llewellyn Publications, 2006.

Kisly, Lorraine, ed. *Watch and Pray: Christian Teachings on the Practice of Prayer*. New York: Bell Tower/Random House, 2002.

Livingstone, E. A., ed. *The Oxford Concise Dictionary of the Christian Church*. New York: Oxford University Press, 2000.

The Methodist Hymnal: Official Hymnal of the Methodist Church. Nashville, TN: Methodist Publishing House, 1964.

O'Malley, Brendan, ed. *Celtic Blessings and Prayers: Making All Things Sacred*. New London, CN: Twenty-Third Publications, 1999.

———, ed. *A Celtic Primer: The Complete Celtic Worship Resource and Collection*. Harrisburg, PA: Morehouse Publishing, 2002.

Shultz, Thomas. *The Rosary for Episcopalians/Anglicans*. Oakland, CA: Regent Press, 2003.

Spoto, Donald. *In Silence: Why We Pray*. New York: Penguin Viking Compass, 2004.

Sweeney, John M. *Praying With Our Hands: 21 Practices of Embodied Prayer from the World's Spiritual Traditions*. Woodstock, VT: SkyLight Paths, 2000.

Tickle, Phyllis. *The Divine Hours: Prayers for Springtime*. New York: Doubleday, 2001.

———. *The Divine Hours: Prayers for Summertime*. New York: Doubleday, 2000.

Webber, Christopher L., ed. *Give Us Grace: An Anthology of Anglican Prayers*. Harrisburg, PA: Morehouse Publishing, 2004.

Wiley, Eleanor, and Maggie Oman Shannon. *A String and a Prayer: How to Make and Use Prayer Beads*. Boston: Red Wheel/Weiser, 2002.

Wills, Garry. *The Rosary*. New York: Penguin Books, 2005.

Zaleski, Philip and Carol. *Prayer: A History*. New York: Houghton Mifflin, 2005.